5

Behavioral Profile
of the
Piano Student

*Including a New Look
at the Cause and Prevention
of Premature Dropouts*

SIDNEY J. LAWRENCE

Preface by
BARBARA JANUARY

WORKSHOP MUSIC TEACHING
PUBLICATIONS
Hewlett, N.Y.

Dedicated
to
GILA *and* YOSEF,
mother and father of my
favorite music-making family:
Daniel, Mimi, Sharona, Jonathan,
Avi, and Hadassi—
and to
Barbara,
Who triggered the writing
of this book. . . .

PUBLICATIONS BY SIDNEY J. LAWRENCE

EVERYONE'S MUSICAL
Psychologically Speaking,
Clayton F. Summy, 1946

A GUIDE TO REMEDIAL SIGHTREADING
FOR THE PIANO STUDENT
A Study In Corrective Teaching Procedures, 1964

THIS BUSINESS OF MUSIC PRACTICING,
Or How Six Words Prevented A Dropout.
Pamphlet, 1968

CHALLENGES IN PIANO TEACHING
One-To-One Lessons For
The Handicapped And Others. 1978

BEHAVIORAL PROFILE OF THE
PIANO STUDENT
Including A New Look At The Cause
and Prevention Of Premature Dropouts.
1978

Sidney Jason Lawrence has served as Director of Research
and Experimentation at the *Neighborhood Music School, N.Y.*
(1939-1950) and *The Harbor Conservatory for Musical
Growth*, Hewlett, N.Y. (1950-   ). Concurrently he held the
post of Head of the Problem Departments of both schools.
Through the 1940's he filled the same capacities at the *Met-
ropolitan Music School*, N.Y.

Contents

Part III
THE INDIVIDUAL CHILD

Part IV
STEPS TOWARD CARRYOVER

Acknowledgments

MY DEEPFELT appreciation to my brother, William Lawrence, for his major editing job on this book—

And my gratitude to the following people who gave so generously of their time to read and edit the manuscript and who contributed with valuable suggestions and constructive criticism:

From the music teachers' point of view—my friends and colleagues, Barbara January, Jacqueline Levine and Neal M. Marcus of the Harbor Conservatory For Musical Growth, N.Y. as well as my daughter, Nadia Dachinger, of the Oceanside District, L.I., N.Y.; from the psychotherapists' point of view—my daughter-in-law, Linda Koffman Lawrence of the North Shore University Hospital, Division of Psychiatrics, L.I., N.Y. and my son Jeffrey R. Lawrence, Clinical Consultant to the Tempo Groups and Psychotherapist in private practice.

And, of course, my wife, Yvette, my dearest critic, who as always, typed countless pages of countless drafts and otherwise contributed to each step of the growth of this book.

Finally, I am indebted to the *Journal Of Research In Music Education* for permission to reprint the article on Carryover, and *The Harbor Conservatory For Musical Growth* for permission to make public the Behavioral Characteristic Report.

S.J.L.

Preface

by BARBARA JANUARY

HOW DOES one learn to teach children to play the piano?

Like so many others in our profession, I simply hung my college diploma over the piano and began to teach. The first lesson I gave was to nine-year-old Jeffrey who had come to me to take his first lesson. We were both beginners and both full of enthusiasm. However, when two hours had gone by and I was still haphazardly relaying information, poor Jeffrey's enthusiasm was on the decline. To my astonishment, Jeffrey returned the following week. I was able to end this lesson at a reasonable time but it was obvious that there was much more to teaching than knowing the subject matter!

I visited several colleges, looking for help, but found that their music curricula were intended for students who had chosen careers as performers, public school music teachers or musicologists. The workshops I attended taught methods which were new and exciting but the courses were too brief and specialized. I began looking for a music school where I could serve an apprenticeship: a place

9

where I could teach and learn at the same time. Finding this kind of school was not easy, but, after several months of searching, a friend recommended the Harbor Conservatory for Musical Growth in Hewlett, N.Y. I made arrangements for an interview and the next day I met Sidney Lawrence.

I found much more than I had hoped for. Mr. Lawrence became my mentor. He was willing to teach me the art of teaching and patient enough to withstand my endless questions and mistakes.

During the first two years under Mr. Lawrence's tutelage, I was, in effect, "de-programmed." It was sometimes painful, but most of the time it was enlightening. For example, we had a rather heated debate about "standards" in music education. I had concluded from my own training that children who study music should strive for excellence, even perfection. Those who met this standard should be rewarded and presented to the less perfect as shining examples of what it means to deserve to take lessons. However, Mr. Lawrence explained that the standards I defended had been established in a misguided attempt to *force* children into a predetermined musical mold. Children, he said, have a natural pattern of growth that applies not only to their physical maturation but to their learning process as well. To expect a child to go beyond his individual, natural pace of learning, or to demand more from him than is possible at a given time, can undermine the child's love for music as well as his self-confidence. The consequence of a teacher's enforcement of these standards and demands is that a child might eventually beg for the lessons to end.

Through discussions like this, I began to understand a philosophy of teaching which is, primarily, concerned with the welfare of the child. A Bach minuet should never receive more consideration than the child who plays it—no matter how poorly he plays it. Even as we try to instill our students with the love of music, as we train their fingers, eyes and ears, as we have them recite the names of the sharps in B-Major, the needs of the *individual* determine how we give a particular lesson and how we set our goals.

Later, after I was appointed Director of the Harbor Conservatory, I had the opportunity to help plan and participate in research and experimental projects under Mr. Lawrence's leadership. Never satisfied that we know enough about music education, Mr. Lawrence continues to search, to analyze, to test new ideas and to report his findings so that everyone can benefit from them.

This book is a guide to understanding children. More specifically, it is a guide to understanding children who are piano students. It is written by a man who has developed extraordinary insights into piano teaching.

Long ago, at that first interview with Mr. Lawrence, I asked him, "How does one learn to teach children to play the piano?" He replied, "You will begin to discover the answers by asking, 'How do children learn?' ".

Behavioral Profile of the Piano Student provides many answers to that question, and an unusual perspective for our consideration: are we primarily concerned with teaching music, or are we primarily concerned with teaching *children*?

It is a valuable book for all of us who love children and love to teach music.

---

*Barbara January has been Director of the *Harbor Conservatory for Musical Growth,* Hewlett, N.Y., since 1972. She is a teacher of teachers, an accomplished pianist, and is author of the method book, *Hello Piano.*

A Note of Explanation

BEHAVIORAL PROFILE OF THE PIANO STUDENT examines the average child from the time he begins piano lessons, at six or seven, to his last years in high school, at sixteen or seventeen. As the subtitle indicates, it also explores the causes of premature dropouts and suggests means for minimizing them.

Two research projects form the basis of this book. The first has recently been completed and is as yet unpublished. Its full title is *AN EXPLORATION OF COMMON BEHAVIORAL CHARACTERISTICS OF PIANO STUDENTS AT EACH AGE LEVEL:* it is actually made up of two separate but related studies. We will call it the DOUBLE PROJECT; it appears in full in Chapter 5. The second project, *FACTORS RELATING TO CARRYOVER OF MUSIC TRAINING INTO ADULT LIFE,* was published in the *Journal of Research In Music Education,* Vol. XV, No. 1 Spring, 1967. It is reprinted in full in the back pages as Appendix and it will be referred to herein as the Carryover Report.

Both projects as well as other studies, surveys and experiments described, quoted or mentioned were mainly conducted by the Research Department of the HARBOR CONSERVATORY FOR

MUSICAL GROWTH, Hewlett, N.Y. and/or THE
NEIGHBORHOOD MUSIC SCHOOL, N.Y.[1] The
original purpose of these projects was to investigate
certain questions which concerned us at those
schools; the results of all experiments and research
were intended to improve our knowledge of student
reaction and learning patterns in order to improve
teaching approaches and pedagogic techniques.

While all projects are limited to obtaining
information related to the specific needs of THE
HARBOR CONSERVATORY, from time to time
it has become evident that the results of certain
projects would be of value to teachers everywhere.
Thus the publication of the aforementioned CAR-
RYOVER REPORT in the J.R.M.E., the book
REMEDIAL SIGHTREADING FOR THE PI-
ANO STUDENT, the pamphlet THIS BUSINESS
OF MUSIC PRACTICING, and other works, were
made available to the entire teaching field.

This particular book, in essence, follows the
rationale and teaching philosophy of THE HAR-
BOR CONSERVATORY.

It is hoped that BEHAVIORAL PROFILE OF
THE PIANO STUDENT will be of interest, practical use and benefit to the private piano teacher,
and through him to the student himself.

S.J.L.

---

[1]THE HARBOR CONSERVATORY FOR MUSICAL
GROWTH, Inc. is a private Music School in Hewlett, N.Y.
It has a student body of over three hundred. The majority of
students consists of those who desire to make music for their
own pleasure. THE NEIGHBORHOOD MUSIC SCHOOL,
a non-profit institution in N.Y.C., sad to relate, closed its doors
in 1970, after serving its community for more than thirty years.

1
Introduction— The Information Gap

IN 1977 MORE THAN 17,000,000 STUDENTS in the United States, ages four to twenty, received instrumental instruction in public schools and with private teachers.[1] Rarely since the days of ancient Greece have parents been so aware of the importance of music-making in the lives of their children. Never before in the history of music education have teachers been so interested in the art and science of teaching those with average ability.

We have not been able to ascertain the actual number of piano students included in the 17,000,000 figure quoted above, but by calculating an estimate based on the 1977 American Music Conference Report, it probably runs over 5,000,000. Since this is a book relating to piano students, we stress this item to make clear we are dealing with a very large proportion of our children population.

---

[1]Report From American Music Conference, 1977.

Recently I mentioned these figures to a group of parents and teachers who were participating in a discussion about children and piano lessons. Everyone, of course, was quite impressed, but one practical-minded parent asked a question which brought about a heated discussion: "How many of them are going to be able to play their instruments when they are grown?"

This led to a debate as to the "why" of music lessons. Some teachers and parents felt that, for the child of average musical aptitude, musical exposure was the essential benefit from music lessons while others felt that the development of disciplines gained from practicing a musical instrument was the prime benefit.

However, the majority of those present would not accept these conclusions. As one parent said, "You don't need *music lessons* for musical exposure, though we agree it can help. There are other ways to get exposure such as music appreciation classes, or taking a child regularly to concerts. While music lessons certainly develop inner disciplines, the latter can also be developed through sports and other such activities. These items beg the real question. Doesn't one take piano lessons in order to learn to play the piano? Though other benefits may be important and welcome they still serve secondary purposes."

According to this concept, it is fair to define a successful piano student as one who has mastered music-making skills sufficiently to make use of them throughout his life. Thus the parent's question is indeed relevant. How many of the 5,000,000 piano students will play as adults?

The answer is dismaying, to say the least. The CARRYOVER REPORT[2] investigated the extent of carryover of music training into adult life. It was found that during the 1930's and 40's only 35% of piano students attained sufficient mastery of piano playing for carryover to adulthood. *Sixty-five percent dropped out of music study before they had attained the necessary skills.* The ratio was even higher with instrumental students.

Does this same ratio hold true today? There are no current statistics available. However with our modern teaching methods and approaches geared toward making music lessons more interesting, together with the latest teaching books and materials aimed at students of limited ambition, discipline and talent, it is highly probable that there is a higher percentage of students achieving carryover. Nevertheless, from our own observations, discussions, and note-comparing with teachers, directors of music schools and parents, we must conclude that even today a great number of students do not attain carryover. At present the ratio may be two out of four or even (but not likely) three out of five. This continues to represent far too high a percentage of students who fail to realize their initial goals.

What are the causes for these failures? Those answers which appear obvious do not stand up under close scrutiny. For example, there are those who believe that dropouts occur simply because the students have reached the point where they have lost interest in music. Among the teachers

---

[2]See Appendix.

and parents who have this opinion are many who are convinced that music is not necessarily for everyone, and that students who drop out should not have been taking lessons in the first place. As an example of the latter type of thinking, some thirty percent of the parents polled in the Carryover Report, gave their children music lessons "as a trial to see if they would take to it". It is small wonder that a number of these children dropped out early, since "taking to it" was usually equated with an unwavering display of interest as manifested solely by constant, self-motivated, enthusiastic practicing, an almost impossible feat for the vast majority of average children.[3]

However, findings in the Carryover Report negate the "interest" explanation. It reports nearly equal percentages of dropouts between students who displayed an enthusiastic interest in music and those whose level of interest fluctuated between casually high to very low. With interested students, practicing was regular, self-motivated and reasonably enthusiastic—yet they suddenly and unaccountably quit their lessons before they had mastered any music-making skills. The students with fluctuating interest practiced erratically, carelessly, hurriedly, often reluctantly, and sometimes not at all. Of course their discontinuance was expected and even encouraged. To make the case even stronger was the evidence that there was also a near equal percentage of students of *both* groups who *continued* on with their lessons until they

---

[3]See Chapter 16, Parental Re-education, concerning actual significance of expressions of "interest" in music.

played the piano sufficiently well for carryover. From these statistics it is apparent that "interest", no matter how defined, has little bearing on whether or not a child prematurely discontinues his lessons.

Other "obvious" explanations for dropouts include economic and/or psychological reasons. There is no doubt that some children do discontinue lessons because the parent can no longer afford to pay for them. Others quit because of inner conflicts, emotional disturbances, etc. However, our own observations with hundreds of students each year indicate that such children comprise a very small part of the total number of dropouts each year.

It would appear that we have come to a dead end—that we cannot ascertain why fifty to sixty percent of piano students discontinue lessons before their training is completed. One possibility, however, bears investigation: we know very little about children's *natural* reactions to music training. How would they normally behave and learn if we didn't impose *our own* values, rules and expectations on them? Until now we have depended upon notions handed down to us which told us how children were expected to respond and to learn at lesson time and at home. These traditional notions have been largely based on the successful experience of the teacher who dealt with the exceptional serious-minded, professionally oriented piano student. There has been no such report concerning the successful experience of dealing with the student of more limited abilities and less ambitious goals. The cold fact is we possess insufficient knowledge about how the average child *really* experiences music lessons and home practicing. This information gap, I believe, has a major bearing on dropouts.

There is considerable evidence that many, if not most, of these dropouts could have been avoided if we knew more about natural behavioral and learning patterns as they pertain to piano training. The purpose of this book is to present such a study of the average piano student. Some material will be documented here for the first time. Combined with well established psychological concepts pertinent to children's learning capacities, the new material forms the author's version of an overview of the piano student—a closer look at his music behavioral profile.

By this means, I hope to help fill in the information gap and give the teacher and the parent new insight into the child himself as he relates to musical development. With that knowledge a more stable foundation can be laid upon which to achieve our initial goal: uninterrupted music training for the child until music-making skills have been mastered to at least a functional level.

PART I
Preliminary
OVERVIEW, TALENT, GOALS

2
Overview

WE TEACHERS KNOW TOO WELL the following story told by a parent: "The teacher tested him and after the first five minutes I was resigned to the fact that Jimmy after all was just a normal, average boy. Well, I consoled myself, at least Jimmy will enjoy music. He will have fun playing the piano. If he will not play at Carnegie Hall, he will at least give little home recitals for his family. I imagined him coming home from the lesson each week, happily whistling the melodies of the pieces he was to practice, and then practicing eagerly and regularly and without question. How much we would all enjoy his music lesson experience!

"Well, it didn't quite work out that way. After a year or so he kept forgetting to practice, I was constantly reminding him. It was getting to be a bothersome chore on both our parts—it was anything but a pleasurable experience. It went on this way—though some weeks were better than others, on the whole it got worse and worse, and finally by the time Jimmy was twelve, he decided to discontinue his lessons. What a waste it had turned out to be! I can't tell you how disappointed I was!"

We teachers are also familiar with the following story: "I can't understand what happened with my student, Jane. Jane is a very talented girl. She was doing very well with her lessons. We had a lovely relationship. She was conscientious and diligent in her home practicing. She mastered her assignments in excellent fashion—scales, exercises, fingering, phrasing, theory, repertoire, all were carefully prepared each week, and I had visions of her going on to become a professional musician. I felt very proud of her. Then suddenly out of the blue, when I least expected it, her work fell down and there was a change in her attitude toward her music and practicing, and our relationship suffered as well. Though I tried everything I could think of in the next number of lessons to bring her back to the path she had been on, nothing helped, and just as suddenly I had a call from her mother telling me Jane had lost interest in music and was quitting."

Both stories are typical of those the author has heard countless times from both parents and teachers. Both stories have one thing in common. They reflect an attitude all of us have shared as far as piano training is concerned. To repeat, we take it for granted that children should develop in and respond to music lessons in a prescribed way. Examine this fact and we see that the unquestioned notion of how the music-education scenario should unravel and unveil itself is *our* (albeit traditionally handed down) version of what ought to take place. Such a scenario is based on *our* values, *our* rules, *our* expectations. Yet what we have failed to see is that despite its traditional acceptance, it simply has not worked for most average students. As Pearce points out: during childhood, parental "anxious intentions" are in conflict with the "biological plan's intent"; the latter drives the child from within, the former presses the child from without.[1]

This then, is what both stories have in common. The parent was disappointed because the child did not (could not?) conform to the parent's "*anxious intentions*". The teacher's bewilderment and dismay also took place because she did not understand the "biological plan's intent" and therefore the child did not (could not?) continue the script the teacher had in mind for her. It is logical to assume that in each case there might have been neither disappointment nor dismay if the parent and teacher had a scenario based on a better understanding of the "biological plan". And both students might have continued on with their lessons!

Thus the two stories bring into focus our need for a more realistic, workable scenario—one based on the biological plan—which would give the Jimmys and the Janes a better chance to continue with music training. To formulate such a script it is necessary first to study the children more fully and then learn to tailor our expectations accordingly.

* * *

At this point we will take the initial step toward increasing our understanding with a general outline of what we have observed in our studies of

---

[1]Joseph Hilton Pearce, Magical Child, N.Y. E. P. Hutton, 1977.

the average piano student throughout his/her years of musical development. This overview is made up of four sections of perspectives, all related to typical and individual responses and behavior:

1. Year by year learning and behavior patterns.
2. The birth order factor.
3. Learning styles.
4. Potential problems.

Of the four sections, the first is by far the most important, if only because its theme is being presented for the first time. Also it covers the largest gap in our understanding of the normal piano student. The following are some preliminary observations:

It takes from five to eight years to learn to play the piano. Of course such a flat statement depends upon one's definition as to what constitutes "playing the piano". In a later chapter we will discuss in detail goals and standards in music lessons. For the time being let us accept the fact that "playing the piano" means sufficient mastery of functional music-making skills by the student. Although bright, well coordinated, well disciplined, and highly motivated students can accomplish this in about five years, most other children will require close to eight years. Children generally start music lessons at eight or nine although some start as early as six. They should continue studying until they finish high school if they wish to achieve sufficient mastery of playing skills.

During these years, the child develops mentally as well as physically. As he grows physically from childhood through puberty into adolescence and on to maturity, he develops mentally from concrete operations to concepts and finally to abstracts. At the same time he is undergoing all sorts of inner chemical changes. We have learned to anticipate shifts in his attitudes and behavior in each developing stage of his growth.

Most of us are aware that such developments take place in all children. However, we have not given this aspect sufficient attention when related to the eight years or so of piano training to be experienced by the student. Therefore the question which looms before us is: how do these developmental changes affect music training?

We will try to answer this question in subsequent chapters by charting the distinctive behavioral and learning patterns at each age level as we discovered them in the double project carried out at the Neighborhood Music School (New York City) and at the Harbor Conservatory For Musical Growth (Hewlett, N.Y.) over a period of some thirty-five years (see chapter on Double Project). We feel that knowledge of dynamic morphology of behavior as related to piano study could affect important changes in the attitudes of both teacher and parent. With such knowledge, the teacher at the lesson will better understand student behavioral reactions and learning responses. The parent (through the teacher) will be more relaxed about home practicing. Finally both teacher and parent will be prepared to anticipate changes in behavior, attitudes and learning patterns likely to take place from year to year.

While the above will indicate the common behavioral and learning patterns from year to year, the remaining three sections in this book will help us understand what is different among children. This should facilitate our understanding of the student as a whole human being. It may appear a contradiction to discuss typical, normal behavioral and learning patterns and at the same time emphasize the fact that each child has different characteristics. However, both Piaget and Montessori argue that an understanding of normal development is a necessary starting point for observing differences in individuals.[2]

Briefly then, to follow the second point in our outline, the birth-order factor relates to the position of the child in the family, in terms of first, second, third, youngest or only child. The position in the family constellation brings about certain personality strengths and weaknesses. These in turn create differences in the way a child reacts to the learning situation and in the way he learns music itself.

In addition, each child develops his own type of learning style, which will depend upon a preferred or favored learning sense. Thus he may learn mainly through the visual senses, the hearing senses, or the kinesthetic and tactile senses. This will also add to individual differences in the way the music student learns.

Finally, there are specific learning, emotional or behavioral problems which may develop in chil-

---

[2]R. C. Orem, Montessori And The Special Child, N.Y., G. P. Putnam's Sons, 1969.

dren from time to time. Obviously, the teacher will need to vary his approach, methods, and in many instances even goals.

To sum up, a study of these last three factors would naturally complement the first factor. It cannot be stressed enough that we must expect individual learning and behavioral reactions as well as typical ones from each child. If the teacher keeps this in mind he will better understand the *whole* child and can help the parent to look upon the child's reaction to music and practicing from a broader point of view.

Before we can proceed with those details, however, it is necessary to clarify two areas which may adversely influence music learning for the average child: we refer to the questions of "musical talent" and "goals". Only if we understand clearly what constitutes talent and how it relates to the average child; and only if we redefine our musical goals can our overview become a basis for effective results.

Therefore, "talent" and "goals" will be examined first.

3
Talent—
What Is It?

IN THE PRECEDING CHAPTER, we have determined that we must not impose our traditional concepts of music learning on the average child. A correlation to this concept is that the child need not show any special talent in order to be eligible for music-making. Thus it becomes apparent that there is a second common point in the two stories mentioned in the last chapter: it relates to the status we give to musical talent, a status which tends to colour and distort our musical goals for the average child. This point is important and bears discussion and reevaluation.

In the one case, the parent fantasized about the possibilities of her son having talent, and was *resigned* "to the fact that Jimmy was after all just a normal, average boy" and *at least* he will "play for the family." As for the teacher in the second story, she mentioned Jane's talent as a special consideration, "Jane is a very talented girl". The assumption appears to be that musical talent is something one either possesses or doesn't. Overlooking the inaccuracy of that assumption for a moment, both attitudes reflect something which could be termed music-chauvanism. There is a kind of eye-brightening "preference" category for the gifted versus a patronizing, condescending air for the "untalented". Of course, no one can fault people for admiring and indeed revering the great musician, or being thrilled to meet a potentially great one, or especially in having a hand in building one, or more especially of dreaming that one's own child might become one, but why equate great artistry or musical professionalism with acquiring musical self-expression? One obvious reason for this unfortunate and unhelpful attitude is that many of us have only a vague notion as to what talent is. Even professional performers and teachers we speak to freely admit they do not know with certainty.

I will state here in unequivocal terms that *everyone has* the capability to make music in some area and to some degree. Our physical selves combined with our mental processes are so arranged that musical expression is as much a part of us as speaking and walking.[1] Today the concept that every child can and should have the opportunity to make music is stressed by our leading pedagogues and music-teaching organizations. For example: "Music for every child, every child for music" is the slogan of the Music Educator's Conference.

What is meant by musical talent? Let us clear

---

[1]Sidney J. Lawrence, Everyone's Musical, Chicago, Clayton F. Summy, pub. 1946.

the air of misconceptions and examine musical talent in relationship to the great artist. In this way we can place it in proper perspective so far as the average music student is concerned.

Many parents believe that their three year old offspring has musical talent if he sings on pitch, rocks his body or beats a drum in rhythmic fashion; or if he pick out tunes on the piano with accuracy. This belief is shared by many teachers as well. Both parents and teachers are also impressed with the child who has "perfect pitch", i.e., the ability to hear a sound and identify it, even though the source of the sound is unseen. Are these indeed indications of musical talent? Before we answer we should try to define the word *talent*.

The dictionary states: "*Talent* is a natural ability, capacity or potential for achievement of success."[2] However, some music psychologists make a fine distinction between *capacity* and *ability*. "*Capacity* has reference to inborn or native power; the term *ability* is used to designate acquired skill in the use of capacity".[3] For the purposes of clarity in this book we shall use the second definition: *talent* is an inborn *capacity* or *potential; ability* is an acquired skill.

Musical talent is further complicated by involving many different kinds of talents, some not necessarily related to music. In short, it consists of a combination of capacities or potentials. The child who sings on pitch, or rocks and uses drumsticks

---

[2]American College Dictionary.

[3]C. E. Seashore, The Psychology of Musical Talent, N.Y., Silver-Burdett, 1919.

rhythmically, or picks out tunes on the piano, or who has perfect pitch, could very well prove to possess considerable talent. However, by themselves, these capacities are not enough. One needs to combine them with still others to become a polished musician.

Seashore describes it this way: "Musical talent is not a single talent, it is a hierarchy of talents, many of which are entirely independent of one another."[4] Schoen agrees that musical talent is made up of a number of capacities: "Talent for music is not a single power or capacity but consists of several groups of talents, each group performing a specific and definite function in the making of the artist. In other words, when the musician works his miracles in his audience through the medium of his voice or instrument, he is exercising not one single power or capacity possessed by him, but a cluster of powers functioning together to produce the single effect."[5]

What then are these groups of aptitudes which, combined, make up the exceptional artist? I believe there are six such groups:

1. "Ear"
2. Physical
3. Reflexes
4. Mental capacities
5. Inner drive
6. Aesthetic

---

[4]Ibid.
[5]Schoen, The Psychology of Music, N.Y. Roseld Press Co., 1940.

A brief explanation of each follows:

First, of course the exceptional artist would have a "musical ear". This means he has the capacity to hear sounds with greater clarity than does the average person. However, having a "musical ear" infers many different faculties, each a talent in its own right. For example, hearing a complicated melody with accuracy is one talent. The combination of both hearing and remembering a tune is another; hearing and repeating rhythms becomes still another facet. Such talents as distinguishing moving harmonies, as well as the quality of tones (timbre), are other capabilities to be reckoned with.

Second, there are physical talents related to music-making. One may have "talented" fingers, i.e., fingers which are built well for the piano (other fingers may be built well for the violin) and which have the potential for great control and facility. The same holds true of hands and arms. This does not mean that all fingers, hands, arms and bodies must be the same shapes or sizes to fit into the "talent" category. Serkin, Horowitz and Rubinstein, to mention three of the great pianists of this century, had very different shapes and sizes: the common factor, however, was that in each case, each part of the body, as well as the body as a whole, was particularly well adapted to music-making.

Third, related to the physical talents, are the all-important reflexes, which are also made up of many aptitudes. These are capacities to use the fingers, hands, arms, eyes and the whole body with incredible speed. These are athletic talents, and one can quickly grasp the kind of potential needed if we think of the great tennis, or football, or baseball star. How he coordinates his physical strength, accuracy of direction and his sense of timing to achieve his particular goal! We know that what the athlete does simply is impossible for the ordinary person. In a like manner, the gifted pianist or violinist combines many reflexes to produce the desired musical effect. We understand that a tennis champion is talented in reflex areas, and we ascribe such a talent to the great musician.

Fourth, there are the mental capacities, e.g., perception, memory, and retention, which are actually tied in with intelligence. Each one is a necessary talent for the great musician.

Fifth, there are the "inner-drive" talents. Briefly, these are inner discipline, single-minded purposefulness, and goal orientation. The capacity for inner discipline is the ability to work with infinite patience on the smallest details, repeating and repeating them, as hours go by unnoticed. There is a compulsive drive to master skills and to complete work, and a dissatisfaction with the results until they are exact. The person with the inner drive can set long range goals with a clear image of each step required to reach those goals. Because of this capacity for drive, nothing deters him from molding that image into something living and real. How many of us are gifted with such drives? There are, undoubtedly, those who will insist that inner drives are learned or acquired characteristics, influenced by emotional and or environmental circumstances. Certainly one or both factors *are* necessary ingredients for such drives to come to life. However, their intensity is completely dependent on the potential there to begin with!

Finally, and probably most important, there are a group of talents whose outline eludes us. They have never been satisfactorily described. These are the talents of the *"aesthetic"*. We cannot define them. We can only describe them in a general way. My own best description, admittedly quite unsatisfactory, is that aesthetic aptitudes are capacities for *feeling* music in a very sensitive way, which is accompanied by the potential to express these feelings through musical rendition so that others may respond to them. For example, the ability to see the Gestalt of a composition, the piece as a whole work and each of its parts in the most logical relationship, would come from an aesthetic aptitude. The ability to shade a phrase, to colour it, in a manner which seems exactly right for it, or to produce sensitive tones which sing in the way the music demands, are other examples of aesthetic capacity.

Are these really inborn aptitudes? Cannot these qualities be learned? Would not these qualities depend upon how well the teacher does his job? The answer is yes, they can be taught just as piano playing can be taught to almost everybody, but only to a certain point. The teachers of Serkin, Horowitz and Rubinstein may have had many other students, some of whom became prominent fine musicians, but none ever equalled these three masters. It would seem logical to conclude that the difference of the degree of inborn talents in people often reflects the difference between the genius and all other performers, assuming each has the same teachers and each applies a similar effort.

Musical talent then is the sum of many components, each an aptitude in its own right. Not one by itself will make a great or even a good musician. The genius probably possesses all of the described capacities in the highest levels[6] while the fine distinguished musician will possess all or most of these qualities at somewhat lower levels and the professional musician will have many of the talents, but probably not all, to still lower degrees.

As for those of us who are not great artists, our fewer and more limited talents are geared to serve totally different but equally important purposes. For us, music-making means self-expression, and not the interpretation of the masters for audiences. Just as we have acquired the skills to read, write and speak in order to fulfill our everyday personal needs and pleasures—and are not concerned with becoming great or professional writers or speakers—so we want to make music, even though our musical accomplishments may rarely raise a critical eyebrow. In the words of J. B. Priestley, writing of the "bad" pianist: " . . but our motives are certainly above suspicion. . Music has no servant more disinterested . . . We gather no garlands in her services . . . The only reward we can hope for is a kindly glance from the goddess of harmony."[7]

---

[6]"Man possesses talent, but genius possessess a man"; Isaac Stern in a TV interview.

[7]Priestley, Essays of Five Decades, N.Y. Atlantic Little Brown, 1968.

The "only reward", as Priestley puts it, is more than enough to fulfill our everyday musical needs and pleasures. Its importance cannot be overstated or overstressed.

I repeat, *everyone possesses sufficient talent to make music.* Everyone *should* make music. However the parent or teacher who is excited about the child who "sings on pitch or rocks his body and beats the drums in rhythmic fashion, or picks out tunes on the piano with accuracy, or indeed has perfect pitch", should not be misled by these single talents. They do not, by themselves, indicate unusual musical talent. It is unfair to ourselves and to the child to harbor and project inflated expectations which may lead him down a dead-end path and out of music altogether. On the other hand, let us not be "resigned" in our attitude toward his "average" talent, anymore than we are "resigned" to the fact that he lacks the ability to be a great actor, athlete, writer, etc.

Remember, "the kindly glance from the goddess of harmony" can bring the average child many rewards in terms of musical self-expression and sheer music-making enjoyment throughout his life.

4
Goals for
the Average Student

THERE ARE TWO WIDELY DIFFERENT
schools of thought concerning goals in music teaching. For one group of educators the primary aim
in music instruction is artistic or aesthetic performance. One needs only to read the countless articles
in such professional journals as Music Educators
Journal, American Music Teacher, or Clavier—all
strongly advocating "Music For Every Child—Every
Child For Music"—and note the emphasis placed on
artistic goals for the student.

At the other extreme there are those teachers
who feel that teaching should not be geared to
artistic results, except in the case of the gifted
student. They feel that music training should be
treated casually, as a hobby. The late Sigmund
Spaeth, for example, believed people should have
fun with music if they did not have sufficient talent
to become professionals or excellent amateurs. He
was convinced that what this country needed, "in

addition to a good five cent cigar", was a lot of "bad" piano players. He felt that practically anyone could find an instrument which would be fun to play—even if only in a haphazard fashion.[1]

A large percentage of the piano teaching materials used today is written by authors who apparently agree with Dr. Spaeth. Among these are primary books written on the basis of a five finger position, containing little pieces which can be played from the first lesson on by virtue of following fingering numbers rather than traditional notation. In addition, there is the current popularity of teaching very simplified arrangements of the latest hit tunes. The huge sales of these books indicate that there are many piano teachers who follow Dr. Spaeth's lead. Between these extreme viewpoints there is no doubt that many teachers have their own modified ideas of teaching purpose.

In my opinion, both schools of thought are somewhat off base. Whether educators speak of aesthetic goals or of simply having fun with music, they are referring to the *quality* of learning rather than the specific ends to be reached by learning. Primary goals should be *skills*. The quality to be attained in those skills is another matter.

While it is true that all skills should be included at one time or another, making the choice remains the most difficult problem. The teacher has a wide variety of skills to choose from as his primary goals. Should he emphasize training in piano fa-

---

[1]Sigmund Spaeth, Fifty Years With Music, N.Y. Fleet Pub. C 1959.

cility, phrasing, tone, technique, memorization, sightreading, improvisation, theory, etc.?

It can safely be said that the goals most important to the student are those skills which he is capable of realizing and which he can utilize in adult life. By that token, those skills which are too difficult to achieve are not going to be of the slightest use to him later on. Furthermore, mastering a skill which would have little utilitarian purpose in later years should not be placed at the forefront of his music-making training.

There is considerable evidence that most amateur musicians in hindsight would have chosen sightreading and improvisation as the preferred skills if they could do it all over again. "At first, during the early lessons, the young student often wants to learn pieces to perform for living room company and friends (something to show for his lessons). He then becomes more practical and desires training in skills which will enable him to accompany the 'gang', as they sing folk songs and hit songs. On the other hand, if he has come to 'accept' the world of more refined music, he might wish to form a little ensemble group. Often he wants to improvise for his own enjoyment. If he has developed aesthetic art values and an appetite for the masters in music, he probably would appreciate an ability to *browse* through the classics of piano literature at will.[2]"

In short, the piano teacher who has at least

---

[2]Lawrence, Remedial Sightreading For Piano Student, Hewlett, N.Y. Workshop Music Pub. 1964.

taught his student to sightread, even in a limited way, and who has helped him develop the basic technique for improvisation, has given that child a foundation to his musical development for the rest of his life.

Once the music teacher has established his goals he may then determine the level of quality to be achieved (which, as we will see, will differ from child to child).

I believe that the terms "artistic" and "aesthetic" apply consistantly to the gifted student but in a very limited way to the average student, only when the student indicates receptiveness.

For the average student we prefer the word "musical" to describe the standard we want to attain. Each piece, whether it is a nursery tune, folk song or the pop ballad, should be played according to its own musical level and with the same spirit it would have if it were sung. Even exercises and simplified excerpts from the classics (stripped as the latter are of the original settings) can be "sung" joyously, or "marched" boisterously, or "whispered" mysteriously.

With the setting of minimum goals and standards, the teacher should not rest there. While the greatest emphasis should be placed on the teaching of functional skills, for the reasons given above, the good teacher will always be making efforts to expand the number of goals, to add more skills to be mastered, and at the same time to bring about a higher standard of playing. He should avoid immediate emphasis on high standards because of the danger of frustrating the student to such an extent that he lose complete interest in music. On the other hand, the teacher ought not to be satisfied to produce a "lot of bad piano players"—although, like Spaeth, this writer would rather see poor musicians than none at all. At all times, the teacher should be feeling his way, probing for the appropriate time to add another skill. Thus he could gradually introduce more of the subtleties of the musical language. This could be accomplished by the addition of an occasional short classic in the original version, eventually introducing longer ones. The dominating purpose of the entire effort should be to gradually increase student interest in playing the masters.

To sum up, then, the primary goals for teaching the piano to the average student are the building of those *functional skills* most likely to carry over into adult life, namely sightreading and improvisation. Our standards should always be musical ones, rather than artistic, keeping in mind that the teacher will constantly be looking for opportune times to add skills, raise standards and ultimately expose the student to the classics when and if he appears receptive.

PART II A

Report:
The Double Project
(Optional Reading)

PART IIA and PART IIB cover essentially the same material. This section documents, in its entirety, the original Report on The Double Project: "An Exploration Of Common Behavioral Characteristics Of Piano Students At Each Age Level." It is published for the first time in these pages, complete with comparative age-level percentages and is presented for the use of those readers who are interested in learning the details of the studies and in examining the evidence on which our conclusions were formulated.

Based on those conclusions, PART II B consists of a projection of a typical child through the years of music development. It also includes suggested teaching techniques for each age level. Readers, if they choose, may skip PART II A and go right on to PART II B without interfering with the continuity of this book.

5

The Double Project

REPORT—AN EXPLORATION OF
COMMON BEHAVIORAL CHARACTERISTICS
OF PIANO STUDENTS AT EACH AGE LEVEL

THIS IS AN UNPUBLISHED REPORT prepared for the use of the faculty of the HARBOR CONSERVATORY FOR MUSICAL GROWTH, Inc., Hewlett, N.Y., which was completed in March, 1976:[1]

Two studies form the basis of this report. The first study was an eight year project undertaken in the 1940's at the NEIGHBORHOOD MUSIC SCHOOL in N.Y. The second study took place in 1975-76 at the HARBOR CONSERVATORY FOR MUSICAL GROWTH, and was undertaken to compare results with the first study.

The first study was longitudinal, lasting from 1941 through 1948. Of the total of twenty students

---

[1]Reprinted in its entirety with permission of the HARBOR CONSERVATORY FOR MUSICAL GROWTH, Inc., Hewlett, N.Y.

involved, two dropped out within the first two years and eighteen completed the project. Tuition fees were covered by a grant from the Neighborhood Music School. The project's purpose was to chart the distinctive behavioral patterns of music students at each age level.

The parents of each child were asked to participate in the following manner: they were not to remind their child to practice at any time, even if the child rarely or never practiced. Their sole involvement with practicing was to take place only when the child asked for help with his assignment, or simply wanted an audience during the practice period. In addition, the parents were asked to report weekly on the extent and quality of the practicing and to observe and report the child's behavior toward the music. Finally and most important they were to report the child's remarks and reactions concerning everything pertaining to music such as the music lessons per se, the teacher, the act of practicing, and music in general.

The teacher's task was to make written observations during each lesson period.

Two teachers participated in the project: Sidney J. Lawrence and the late Esther Kleinfeld, both faculty members of the school. The findings were documented annually, reported, and discussed at hundreds of music teachers forums and parent organization meetings throughout New York State.

The second project was a horizontal one, started in the fall of 1975 and completed in the spring of 1976. Its purpose was to check the general conclusions of the initial study, and to add any further findings which had developed, and to ascertain, within the limitation of a small study, whether in the thirty years which had lapsed between the studies, children's timetable of behavior had changed in any way. Other influences to be considered were economic and environmental. Economically the children in the first project were of lower income. Those of the second group were more affluent though of similar ethnic and cultural background.

Eighty children and seven teachers were involved in the second project. The teachers were Barbara January, Jacqueline Levine, Joanne Levy, Rosalie Kopman, Barbara Goldstein, Neal M. Marcus and Sidney J. Lawrence, all of the faculty of the HARBOR CONSERVATORY FOR MUSICAL GROWTH, Hewlett, N.Y. The students, ranging in age from six to sixteen, were selected from the assigned students of the participating teachers. A questionnaire was prepared based on the results of the first study. The teachers observed these children's behavior and reactions during lesson periods using the questionnaire as a guide. They checked those characteristics which agreed with their own observations, writing 'no' or leaving blank those with which they didn't agree, and finally adding new observed characteristics not listed. One teacher was given permission to omit the questionnaire entirely and to limit her report to her own observations. Finally, a list of these added observations were sent to all the teachers, who verified them by further observing their students with the new characteristics in mind. In this way the complete list of characteristics was formulated.

Special note: the parents of the children in the second study did not participate. All conclusions were made exclusively from teachers observations. Obviously, these students practiced at home under different conditions than did those of the initial study: their parents *did* remind them to practice from time to time, sometimes rewarding them, sometimes punishing them, sometimes being permissive. Thus the results of the current study were derived under "normal" conditions. In contrast, the results of the initial study were obtained solely from the students' self-generated work. It was hoped in this way to double-check the conclusions.

The breakdown of the various results follows on a stage-to-stage basis.

COMPARISONS
SIX-SEVEN YEAR OLDS

	Initial Study (Out of 20 children) (Longitudinal)		*Current Study* (Out of six children) (Horizontal)	
1. Loves music lessons	20	100%	6	100%
2. Loves teacher	20	100%	6	100%
3. Tends to be attracted to single unrelated notes	13	66%	4	66%
4. Two hand coordination is difficult	18	90%	5	80% app.
5. Memorizes quickly	18	90%	2	33%
6. Eager to practice	17	85% app.	4	66%
7. Practices erratically	16	80%	5	80%
8. Likes to play before audience	18	90%	5	80%
9. Often wants parental supervision	16	80%	0	No parental reports
10. Can pick simple melodies by ear	8	40% app.	0	
11. Very short attention span	18	90%	4	66%
12. Resists note reading	17	85% app.	4	66%
13. Likes variety of little pieces			5	80%
14. Doesn't like to repeat			4	66%

In general, the longitudinal and horizontal studies check with each other. Apparently, the child of this age loves music, idolizes his music teacher and is eager to practice, but has not yet developed work discipline, has a short concentration span and is still uncoordinated. Thus he practices erratically and briefly at that.

COMPARISONS
EIGHT YEAR OLDS

	Initial Study (Out of 19 children) (Longitudinal)		*Current Study* (Out of 11 children) (Horizontal)	
1. Loves lessons	19	100%	11	100%
2. Loves teacher	19	100%	11	100%
3. Has begun to relate sounds	10	55% app.	6	60% app.
4. Two hand coordination improved somewhat	16	85% app.	10	90% app.
5. Dawdles and day-dreams now	12	65% app.	6	65% app.
6. Fidgets a great deal	6	30% app.	2	33%
7. Resists note reading	15	75% app.	6	65% app.
8. Is not as eager to practice as he used to be—practices very little	14	75% app.	2	20% app.
9. Memorizes quickly	13	20% app.	8	80% app.
10. Likes to play before audience	14	75% app.	7	60% app.
11. Practices eagerly			7	60%
12. Practices daily			5	55% app.
13. Longer attention span (than sixes and seven)			4	35% app.
14. Works diligently			7	60% app.
15. Likes parental guidance			7	60%

While almost all items of the longitudinal and horizontal studies agree, there are two areas which, on the surface, appears to be diametrically opposed in each study. First there is Item 8, second there are the new items 11 to 15. Combined, these items indicate a reversal of findings. However, there is one important fact not yet stated: of the eleven students observed in the horizontal study, only three had studied at seven—the rest were absolute beginners. More about this later.

In the longitudinal study we have evidence of a drop in music interest and drive as compared to the same child at six and seven. The eight year old dawdles and fidgets and daydreams and often "acts up" at the lesson, though he has begun to relate sounds and is somewhat better coordinated. He has no desire to practice even to the extent he used to, though he does not want to give up his lessons. Thus, the Eight year old tends to show a drop in interest and drive in music lessons, as compared to Six-Seven.

In the horizontal study, however, we see that less than 20% experience such a drop (Item 8). Moreover, from the evidence in Items 11 to 15, we see much the opposite: "practices eagerly—60%," "practices daily—60%" "works diligently—60%." Before we jump to the conclusion that the new generation of eight year olds is totally different from the old generation, we must remember that eight of these children were absolute beginners. Only three had had music lessons at seven, and of the three, two followed the same patterns of behavior as those in the longitudinal study. However, the difference of behavior of those who were beginners raises an interesting question: could it be that starting at eight eliminates the drop that seems almost inevitable for children who start at seven? Would the children in the longitudinal study have skipped the drop had they started a year later? If so, the policy of the Harbor Conservatory (emphasizing pre-instrument classes at seven, and piano lessons at eight) would seem to be justified. In any case, here is a point of investigation to be considered for future projects.

COMPARISONS
NINE-TEN YEAR OLDS

		Initial Study (Out of 19 children) (Longitudinal)		Current Study (Out of 25 children) (Horizontal)	
1.	Tends to play physically rather than musically	15	70% app.	18	72% app.
2.	Often plays as fast as possible	16	80% app.	18	72% app.
3.	Is apt to be very careless with time values, fingering, etc.	14	75% app.	19	75% app.
4.	Improved two hand and finger coordination	18	95%	22	90% app.
5.	Is less likely to be confused by notation rhythm division	17	90% app.	21	80% app.
6.	Likes to play for his peer (but not for grownups)	11	60% app.	15	60%
7.	Accepts practicing as responsibility	14	75% app.	18	72% app.
8.	Will practice from 20 to 45 minutes daily	14	75% app.	0	
9.	Will practice 15-25 minutes daily			20	80%
10.	Progresses evenly and steadily			18	72% app.
11.	Easily frustrated			11	40% app.

In our comparison between the longitudinal and the horizontal studies we find almost complete verification. Several changes have taken place in the nine-ten year olds. He has recovered from the "eight year old drop" in interest and inner discipline. He practices with more enthusiasm or at least he accepts his responsibility readily now. He will play musically and follow directions carefully if he is in the hands of a teacher who inspires him. His musical playing will almost always be imitative. However, his natural tendency is to play for the physical pleasure of it. Left to his own resources his playing would be mechanical, without much regard for wrong notes, fingering or rhythm. Speed is his greatest joy. "Look how fast I can play it!" appears to be his favorite goal. The modern child will practice fairly regularly but apparently only about half as long as the child of thirty years ago. This may be due to the economic differences between the two groups, i.e., do children from lower income areas tend to practice longer? Or is it due to the television influence, i.e., since T.V. now takes up a great deal of a child's time? At any rate, these are points worth investigating in another study.

COMPARISONS
ELEVEN YEAR OLDS

	Initial Study (Out of 18 children) (Longitudinal)		*Current Study* (Out of 23 children) (Horizontal)	
1. Likes technical playing	9	50%	10	40% app.
2. Two clef eye-hand coordination improved	12	66%	14	60% app.
3. Still plays carelessly	10	55% app.	13	60% app.
4. Still likes to play fast	10	55% app.	11	50% app.
5. Tends to play loud	10	55% app.	11	50% app.
6. Likes pop music and or jazz	16	90% app.	20	90% app.
7. Likes to improvise	14	75% app.	16	65% app.
8. Often wants music too advanced	6	33%	6	28% app.
9. Dislikes playing before audience	6	33%	7	30% app.
10. Practices diligently	5	30% app.	10	45% app.
11. Practices spasmodically			9	40% app.
12. Will practice only what he or she likes			16	65% app.
13. Has definite opinions about music			8	35% app.
14. Frightened by pieces that look too hard			10	45% app.
15. Does not like long projects			14	40% app.
16. Easily frustrated			9	40% app.
17. "I want to quit"			6	28% app.

The eleven year group in many ways is an extension of the nine-ten year level. However, there are definite signs of changes taking place which will develop into problems later on. The tendency for speed and carelessness is still there and, in addition, many of these students tend to play continually loud.

The eleven year old has begun to have very definite opinions. Now he likes to play popular music and sometimes jazz, and he likes to improvise. He wards off serious music unless the teacher can find pieces which have a special appeal to him.

He is easily frustrated, avoiding music which looks "too hard" and he does not like long projects, i.e., pieces which take many weeks, or months to learn.

The first signs of the "I want to quit" syndrome appears.

At this age level, the comparison between the initial study and the current one is in need of special explanation. As the figures clearly indicate, a majority of students in the initial study (65%) wanted to quit their music lessons at this time. Of course, they didn't because of the agreement at the start of the project to continue lessons under all circumstances. In addition to the desire to quit, many of these students practiced with hostility, or avoided practicing altogether, or practiced only what they liked to play. Many were easily frustrated when learning did not come easily and at the same time resisted all corrections from the teacher. All in all, in this group, one sees a decided down trend in attitudes toward music, a very negative picture, indeed. Only about 30-35% still enjoyed music-making. Over the years, since the initial project was completed,

COMPARISON
TWELVE-FIFTEEN ADOLESCENCE

		Initial Study (Out of 18 subjects) (Longitudinal)		*Current Study* (Out of 15 subjects) (Horizontal)	
1.	Has very definite likes and dislikes in music	16	85% app.	9	60%
2.	Wants latest peer (pop) music	10	55% app.	8	55% app.
3.	Willing worker and practices well	7	40% app.	12	80%
4.	Has eye-hand coordination difficulties	5	28% app.	8	55% app.
5.	Loves to play	7	40% app.	10	66%
6.	Would like to play well without practicing	14	75% app.	0	
7.	Practices erratically	9	50%	4	30% app.
8.	Practices with hostility	9	50%	—	(No report from parents
9.	Avoids practicing altogether	9	50%	—	" "
10.	Practices only what he likes	13	70% app.	3	20%
11.	Easily frustrated	14	75% app.	3	20%
12.	Resists correction	9	50%	1	
13.	"I want to quit"	11	65% app.	0	

teachers everywhere have verified these findings, and today it is accepted as inevitable that most students will develop hostile feelings toward music lessons and most of these will quit somewhere between the ages of 13 and 15.

Why then, in the current study, do we see such totally different results? Out of the fifteen subjects at this age *none* wanted to quit. None showed hostility or avoided practicing. Eighty percent were willing workers. Sixty-six percent still loved to play. Do not these figures disprove the results of the initial study?

Actually, as we shall see, these figures *verify* the results of the initial study. Keep in mind the current study is a horizontal one, whereas the

initial study is longitudinal. The reason for the smaller drop in the current study is found in the unusual policy followed by the Harbor Conservatory For Musical Growth. Thanks to the information we had obtained in the initial study, we do everything in our power to keep the student at his piano during this stage. Many times this works and the student—and teacher—continues on.*
When it doesn't work, the student is encouraged to switch instruments, usually the guitar. In short, while the same percentage of students *want* to quit, most of them either elect to continue with piano or change instruments. Therefore, the dropout rate is much smaller at the Harbor Conservatory and the figures actually indicate the number of students who *remain* with piano. The would-be dropouts were playing other instruments and of course were not included in the survey.

We conclude, therefore, that the current study verifies the initial one.

We believe that while our list is correct, it is probably incomplete and there is no question but that much needs to be done in the way of research and exploration in this direction.

The most significant information to come out of the Double Project was a verification of what many music educators had suspected for years. Most children follow a zig-zag curve in the course of their piano study, and the same zigs and zags occur at the same age level for the majority of children. Therefore, we must conclude from the

*For further details on the approach used here see chapter: "Lisa in Adolescence".

study that the child's musical development does not progress uniformly from year to year.

Note that the above comparative lists indicates that progress is sometimes forward, sometimes sideways, occasionally coasts downhill and may abruptly come to a dead halt. There are high points of enthusiasm and low points of lethargy and, most important, there are different stages during which the student will respond best to specific areas in music training.

The highest points of enthusiasm come when lessons begin, at seven or eight or nine, but not again until the student is sixteen or seventeen. If the child began his lessons at six or seven, the lowest points appear at eight when there is much lethargy, and then again during adolescence when there is rebellion and hostility. Nine and ten year olds tend to be physical and mechanical about music, and at eleven the student becomes peer-sophisticated.

Sixes, sevens and eights like learning about individual sounds and they resist note-reading, but they like learning about rhythm-clapping. Nines and tens like learning to read music, learning techniques such as staccato and legato and especially very rapid playing. Eleven feels closest to the popular songs of the day and will be drawn to learning how to use chords. The challenge of improvising music has great appeal to children who are twelve or over. Finally those students who continue studying at sixteen and seventeen love to make music because of the sheer pleasure of playing an instrument.

PART II B

Projection—
the Story of Lisa

Based on the Double Project, and using case histories from my personal files, in this section I have projected a hypothetical child and we follow her in her music training from the age of six-seven through sixteen-seventeen.

The last pages of each chapter will deal with general suggestions for teaching approaches and techniques which could apply to the developmental uniqueness of the particular age level. They should be supplemental to the teacher's individual methods.

6
Lisa at Six-Seven

LISA IS A COMPOSITE of most boys and girls
at each level. She is typical and representative in
her music reactions and development.

At six and seven, Lisa's most striking music
characteristic is her constant craving for playing
the piano. Every day, she persistently asks her
mother for piano lessons. The desire is apparently
not simply a whim, but a kind of hunger. She
eyes every piano she sees, with longing. She is
envious of those of her friends who have already
started lessons. Finally, when her parents do buy
a piano, she is constantly playing, picking out
tunes like "Hot Cross Buns", and "Mary Had a
Little Lamb", note by note, with intense concentration and delight.

Once the piano lessons have started, she is in
heaven. Throughout the week, she eagerly and
impatiently awaits her next lesson. She loves them,
is extremely alert and avidly absorbs each new bit
of learning, enjoying every moment of contact
with her teacher. In short, she rides on a high

plane of musical pleasure, receiving a kind of satisfaction she is not likely to again experience until she is sixteen or seventeen.

One of the great pleasures she receives is from single isolated tones. She will pick the tone *A*, for example: "I love that sound! It is a pretty sound!" or, she will exclaim about another tone, "I don't like that sound, it is ugly!" She doesn't yet hear tones as related to one another, but rather each as a complete unit in itself with its own characteristics and uniqueness.

Practicing is not accomplished without difficulties. She really does not know how to practice and is actually not ready to concentrate in an organized manner. Both parent and teacher do not object because Lisa is at the piano often, though not for long periods—perhaps two to three minutes at a time. Although she may forget to practice on occasion, her general attitude is so joyful and enthusiastic that this seems ample dividend for the investment in music lessons.

She memorizes her little pieces quickly and loves to play for audiences. At the drop of a hat she will perform for all company, will visit all of the neighbors who have pianos and display her achievements complete with announcement and bows, playing proudly and with a watchful eye for applause.

However, her learning capacity does not match her enthusiasm at this age level. She resists note-reading. Space concepts are still developing and reverse images are still confusing. Her eyes do not yet focus long enough to "see" five staff lines for each hand. The result is the "hieroglyphics" on them are often bewildering. In large part, she learns to play the piano by rote. This can inhibit her ability to read music later on, a problem which will be discussed in later chapters.

While her individual finger control is developed well enough to play simple songs on the piano, she often finds the coordination of playing two hands together overwhelming. However, in another year or two, she will tend to overcome this problem.

Her attention span is short. The skilled teacher will understand this as a typical age-level characteristic and keep Lisa's interest by artfully sensing when it is time to leave one subject and move to another. This can occur several times within the lesson.

To sum up, Lisa at six-seven loves music, adores her teacher and has much fun with music at home. She has not yet developed practice discipline, has a short concentration span, and is still uncoordinated. She resists note reading, but likes to play by rote. Gesel and Ilg touched upon music lessons in their research and made this comment: "Seven often may express a strong desire to take piano lessons. The question may be asked whether the craving should be satisfied. It probably is desirable to satisfy the demand if the music teacher will allow the child to take lessons without practicing, which is often the preferred way to learn".[1]

---

[1] Arnold Gesel, Frances L. Ilg. et al, The Child From Five To Ten, N.Y. Harper and Bros. Pub. 1946.

TEACHING PROCEDURES

Many piano teachers feel that piano lessons are not desirable at this age. The average six or seven year old has not yet fully established such concepts as right-left handedness, reversibility (thinking the alphabet and numbers in reverse when required) pitch relationships and direction, etc. In addition, the child's small motor control probably has not yet reached the required level of maturity. Therefore, the advisability of children of this age beginning private piano lessons is questioned.

Instead, they feel it is more desirable to place the child in a situation where he can *prepare* for the study of an instrument and at the same time satisfy his hunger to make music. There are special pre-instrument classes designed for just these purposes. There are classes in Orff work, Dalcroze, Kodaly, Carabo-Cone and many others. Any of these better serve the six-seven year old because in such a class he will develop the necessary concepts as well as his small motor control. By the time he is eight or nine, he should be ready, indeed, for piano lessons.

For those who do teach the six-seven year old on a one-to-one basis the following teaching procedures are recommended to offset the above mentioned disadvantages:

1. For gross motor development:
    a. Body movement to teacher's playing, utilizing legs and arms.

    b. Clapping in rhythm.

    c. Rhythmic shorthand, i.e., clapping to half notes, whole notes, etc., that are placed before the student.

2. For pitch direction:

    a. Drills on reversibility: reciting the alphabet to G and backward from G to A. Reciting numbers to ten and backward from 10. What comes after G in music? What comes before A?

    b. Singing songs with hands moving in space following the same direction and contours taken by the melody.

3. For laterality:

Which is right hand, which left hand? Some identifying object such as a ribbon or rubber band should be placed on the right arm.

7
Lisa at Eight

AS LISA TURNS EIGHT, her teacher and parent are dismayed to note a negative change in her attitude toward music. In her social and educational areas the changes taking place in Lisa are more positive. She is forming and joining clubs in an awakening interest in her peers. She is beginning to read fairly well in school and is interested in a wide variety of subjects, such as books dealing with other countries, mechanical things, games, etc. Nevertheless, her former enthusiasm and her year-old love of music apparently have vanished.

Lisa insists she still loves music and the piano, but apparently does not feel as attracted to either as she did at Seven. She still loves her teacher, but does not need his approval as she did at Seven. While still wanting to go to her lesson, she spends her time alternately dawdling, daydreaming and fidgeting. The teacher often wonders if any of the subjects he is emphasizing are seeping through. A few months later, the instructor will be surprised to observe that much of the material has penetrated as if by osmosis.

Lisa practices infrequently, usually when a parent sits with her. She postpones practicing when reminded, with a promise to do it later, and then forgets her promise. When, eventually, under pressure, she does sit down to practice, she avoids her music assignment, experiments with "Heart and Soul" or focuses her attention on experimenting with her music assignment "to see how it sounds".

She still memorizes easily, when she does practice, and still likes to play for audiences, but more self-consciously, since she is not sure she knows the music well enough.

Because she is older, her learning potential should show improvement. Unfortunately, at this stage she is not ready to apply herself even though her sense of concepts should have developed to a greater degree. Her eyes should focus better and for longer periods than before. Yet she still avoids learning notation. Her two hand coordination is expected to be much further developed than it was at Seven, still she avoids two hand playing. Although her ear is better attuned, since she now hears notes related to one another rather than the individual note possessing its own set of characteristics, she is not inclined to make use of this developing ability except when she is picking songs out by trial and error. As a result, all these expected improvements have not materialized because Lisa's enthusiasm for music seems to have almost vanished. Gesel et al notes: "The initial seven year old flare of interest in music may die

out unless someone plays with the child or sits
with him while he plays. He enjoys playing duets.
Practicing cannot be forced and often it is wise
to interrupt lessons for a while until he is ready
to return at a later date (Nine-Ten)."[1]

On the other hand, Lisa has several friends
of both sexes, also turned eight, who have just
started piano lessons. They are enthusiastic, practice with gusto, and have better discipline than
Lisa did at Seven. Two of them do even better
than the rest since they had training in classes
(mentioned in Chapter 6) for two years prior to
private lessons.

Hence, for Lisa, Eight represents a drop in
musical interest. The fact that her friends are
enthusiastic about music lessons indicates that Eight
may be a wiser time than Six or Seven to begin
piano lessons, thus avoiding the Eighth year drop.
The fact that her two friends who have had pre-
instrument training made so much better progress
than the others is evidence that starting such classes
at Six or Seven and beginning private lessons at
Eight may be the ideal way to launch a music
education.

TEACHING PROCEDURES

1. Duets, as much as possible, between child and
   mother (if she plays) or teacher.
   All other procedures should continue as in Six-
   Seven.

---

[1]Gesel, Child From Five To Ten, Ibid.

2. Body movements to teacher's playing.
3. Singing songs with hands moving in space following direction and contours of melody.
4. Clapping to rhythm shorthand.
5. Drills on reversability (reciting alphabet letters to G forward and backward. Same with numbers to ten. Drill on what comes after *G* in music, what comes before *A* in music?)
6. Which is right hand, left hand? Keep identifying mark on one hand, e.g., rubber band around right hand.

8
Lisa at Nine and Ten

BOTH TEACHER AND PARENT are surprised and delighted to see a difference in Lisa at age nine. In general they note that she is acquiring a new form of self-dependence, of looking at the world with wide curious observing eyes. Her relations with her peers, her school, her parents and her music teacher, are taking on a new aspect. She has begun to take the measure of herself and those around her. This new attitude is reflected in a change in her music-learning and practice habits. So far as the piano is concerned, Lisa has shed her eight-year-old-doldrums and has become an interested, eager, and in certain areas, a self-motivated student.

Lisa has become more adept at finger and hand movements. Her two-hand and eye-hand co-ordination have matured and no longer require labored effort. She is capable of reading notation now, with the ability to see all of the staff lines clearly and in relation to one another, and is educable so far as vertical two clef reading is concerned. Her mind can grasp rhythmic division and dynamic signs. In short physically and mentally, she is ripe for a period of mastering skills and absorbing information. It could be one of the most productive learning periods in her life.

Lisa accepts the chore of practicing now as a fact of life. She neither loves nor does she hate it. She simply approaches it in a business-like fashion. It is part of her daily routine similar to her homework. Sometimes she must be reminded to practice and other times she may neglect it altogether. However, she does *intend* to practice, and sooner or later she will accomplish it. Such incidents are not an indication that she is "losing interest" in music. It merely suggests that in her growing sense of being organized, other interests have taken priority.

Lisa has improved her concentration habits at the piano. She can practice for longer periods and work with undivided attention.

However, there is a new aspect to Lisa's change of attitude toward her piano playing. The nine-ten year old Lisa tends to feel her music in a *physical* way—she enjoys the mechanical movement, the kinesthetic sensation, the athletic satisfaction of muscles in action. Stunts are a challenge to her; speed appeals to her; she is apt to exclaim: "Look, Ma, with my eyes closed!" or "Look, Ma, listen to how fast I can play this!" Physical power and energy are her driving forces.

While this new approach is not likely to be pleasing to either teacher or parent, it is probably very important to her overall growth and development in music. Her new interest in music is quite a contrast to that of her six-seven year old period when she *felt* sounds in terms of joyful experience and took a keen delight in little nursery tunes.

Thus, while Lisa can concentrate better than ever before, her practice habits are governed by motives often at odds with her music teacher's goals. Lisa is consumed with an impatience to finish each piece so that she can start the next one as soon as possible. She is not concerned with a special effort to achieve correct notation, fingering and rhythm. As a result she is apt to be careless in her playing to the exasperation of both parent and teacher. On the other hand, she is likely to be quite aware and proud of her presto tempi.

Sensitive playing is rarely a self-motivated characteristic at this age. If it is attained, it is through strong persistent teaching. In these exceptional cases, as excellent as the results may appear to be, they are likely to be more imitative than a genuine expression of feeling.

Lisa loves to play for her peers. She is not self-conscious. She plays freely, disregards mistakes and proudly displays her latest accomplishment in speed. By contrast, she is reluctant to play for family and relatives and only does so after much coaxing.

In sum, Nine and Ten prove to be quite fruitful learning years for Lisa, but usually not in accordance with the expectation of teacher and parent. Finger facility, reading of music, eye-hands (and pedal foot) coordination are the type of skills which can develop and grow in Lisa. Musical sensitivity can be nurtured to some extent, but rarely in response to inner motivation, or to fulfill a music-making need.

TEACHING PROCEDURE

The author is convinced that students like Lisa feel "physical" musical urges in response to the natural "biological plan" of musical development. Nine-Ten, then, is primarily a period of expanding kinesthetic/tactile awareness, necessary to nature's long range design. For this reason, our own concerns for growth in inner discipline and work habits are given little attention by the nine-ten year old. She (or he) neither understands nor knows how to attain what we expect of her; one cannot blame her for wanting to "do what comes naturally".

The teacher is thus faced with the dilemma of how to guide the student to higher levels of work habits without stunting growth and enjoyment of piano playing, or suppressing satisfaction of kinesthetic/tactile urges. It can be done with a careful empathetic approach and the following recommended procedure:

Step 1. Rhythm and tempo control—before playing each etude or composition, clap and count the rhythm *away* from the piano, each clef separately.

Step 2. For notation and fingering accuracy—
    A. Before playing an etude or composition *play each hand mentally away from the piano*—visualizing with great care, fingering, key signature and accidentals repeated within a measure.
    B. Then play the etude or composition on the piano.

Urge the student to follow this two step procedure at home during practicing, before each playing (most nine-ten year olds find this fun).

Imaginative games, suitable for this age level, can effectively re-enforce the establishment of these habits. For example, to re-enforce the control of fingering and finger posture, Barbara January, Director of the Harbor Conservatory, recommends the following game called Coach and Players. The mind is the coach of the ten man team, each finger is a player on the team. The coach (student) gives direction to the fingers as to what each one will be expected to do. Of course, each player (finger) wants to be a good team player, so it will learn its assigned role. The student is thus made aware of each individual finger's part, and is mentally prepared to have it play the correct keys.

The above suggestions not only effectively improve inner discipline and work habits, they also satisfy the "physical" urges more fully than before. Mental playing involves "imaginary" use of fingers, hands, and arms and thus strengthen the kinesthetic/tactile sense.

Finally, duets and ensemble playing should be emphasized during this period. Usually such activities, by their built-in pressures to play in rhythm, help bring home to the student the importance of greater attention to details.

9
Lisa at Eleven

THE ELEVEN YEAR OLD STAGE for Lisa appears at first to be an extention of her Nine-Ten period. However, as time goes by, it is apparent that changes are taking place. Lisa thinks she is more sophisticated now; tries to act more adult; becomes skeptical of the grownups around her; begins to question authority, and in general gives clear indications that she wants to learn about life in her own way, with minimum adult direction.

This attitude affects her music-learning. Lisa's eager outlook shows signs of waning. While she continues to make excellent progress as before in mastering music skills, the pace has become irregular; the work is not quite as business-like as before; uneasy situations crop up here and there.

While Lisa appears to practice much as she did in the past, there are differences, subtle at first, then becoming quite marked as the months go by. She will practice diligently, but suddenly there will be a period when she is less accepting about it. At first this does not last long, but it will come again and again, each period lasting for a longer interval, occasionally accompanied by flashes of resistance and anger.

In her playing, Lisa still thinks in the terms of the physical. Fast playing apparently continues to be an objective for her, but now it is more often than not coupled with *loud* playing. The loudness itself is perhaps an indication of protest. She still pays little attention to wrong notes and is almost oblivious to fingering. However her signs of dissatisfaction are perhaps evidence that she is beginning to be aware that something is missing in her playing, after all.

Lisa has become quite definite about the music she wants to learn. She has become very much aware of popular music, and often seems to believe that a current "Top Forty" is the only music in existence. Lisa has begun to ask, sometimes to insist, that popular music be assigned to her to learn. Whether this is an indication of growth in musical discrimination (the very act of desiring *any* specific style of music indicates selectiveness), or of simply following the taste set by her peer groups, is difficult to say. Consequently, Lisa now tends to scoff at and act scornfully towards music with which she is not very familiar. She sometimes limits her practicing to those pieces she likes and simply disregards the rest of her assignment, much to her teacher's frustration.

From time to time Lisa's manner is contra-dictory. She says, "I want long hard grown-up pieces, this is too babyish". She then proceeds to select a composition far too difficult for her. But because she is impatient with long projects, she quickly gives it up. On the few occasions that she determinedly perseveres to the end, she is quite satisfied with a careless, sloppy performance. On the other hand, Lisa is often frightened by pieces which "look too hard," even though the teacher is convinced the selections are well within her capacity. Sometimes, Lisa, frustrated by her inability to easily master a selection which she is anxious to learn, demonstrates her frustration by banging on the piano with both fists.

Occasionally, after an unsatisfying practice session she will say: "I don't think I like to play the piano any more", and will speak of quitting her lessons. However she quickly changes her mind.

Lisa will not play for anyone now, not even her peers; she simply becomes too self-conscious and nervous before an audience.

To sum it up, then, Eleven is a year which continues to represent solid growth in music-making development, in spite of her new resistance. The net result is a slower although erratic rate of progress when compared to the Nine-Ten year stage. This slowdown is undoubtedly due to the changes taking place in Lisa. Through her changing behavior, one can clearly see the roots of adolescence taking hold and can anticipate the path their growth will take. The beginnings of the need for peer acceptance, the occasional flashes of resistance and anger directed at adults and those in authority, and the growing impatience with herself as displayed by the moments of frustration are all the first signs which foretell the nature of things to come for Lisa.

TEACHING PROCEDURES

Introduce the building of chord symbols and apply them to playing the popular music of the day, in addition to regular curriculum.

The two step procedure of Nine-Ten should be continued:

1. Rhythm and tempo control—for each etude and composition, clap and count rhythm away from the piano before each playing.
2. For notation and fingering accuracy—play each hand mentally before playing (away from keyboard) with special attention to correct notes, fingering, key signature, accidentals repeated in measure, etc.

Duets between students, introduce accompanying other instruments.

10

Lisa at Twelve to Fifteen—
Adolescence

BETWEEN TWELVE AND FIFTEEN Lisa goes
through a difficult stage indeed. In the eyes of
both parent and teacher, the ominous signs of
Lisa's eleventh year have grown into full fledged
adolescent "problems", something today's parent
has been taught to anticipate. The parent knows
that the adolescent child is in constant conflict
between retaining the security of childhood and
the eagerness to assert independence in her role
as adult. Thus she observes Lisa undergoing inner
upheaval and turbulence. She finds herself constantly dealing with Lisa's resistance to authority
and with Lisa's rebellion against the set rules of
home, school and society. Even though the parent
manages to "keep Lisa in line", it is a difficult
and often nerve-wracking task.

Surprisingly, music has taken on a new meaning and importance in Lisa's life. This takes the

form of the "hit" songs of the day. From morning till night, Lisa devotes hours listening to music on the radio; she plays current records of her favorite rock or folk or country western singer, sings the newest songs over and over again, and eagerly plans to attend concerts where her singing idols will appear. Observing Lisa, one cannot help comparing her love for rock music to that of the aficionado of "serious" music: there is a similar earnestness and devotion. No doubt about it, Lisa loves music now as she never loved it before. It is not important that she cares only for one type of music and resists accepting musical tastes "dictated" to her by adults or society in general. This is *her* music, and Lisa would suffer emotionally if it were taken away from her.

In spite of the overpowering love for song and rhythm, she has a negative reaction to her piano lessons. Lisa has begun to "hate" practicing. She no longer likes to play the piano. Her relationship with her music teacher, whom she adored through the years has started to deteriorate. Why should she be "forced" to practice, when she is not interested in the boring music assigned to her? As a result she practices very little. Even if the music is to her liking, she is "too busy" to practice, and avoids it. She finds the piano itself "boring". Since most of her friends have quit their lessons because of boredom why should she have to play? These attitudes manifest themselves in a negative reaction to her teacher's corrections and suggestions. At lesson time, she is usually hostile and defiant, sullen and silent, and playing, as one colleague put it, with her "resistance showing".

Like her friends, Lisa wants to discontinue her lessons. She maintains a constant campaign on this theme with her parents who are at a loss to know how to deal with the problem. They are strongly tempted to yield, following the example of the great majority of the parents of Lisa's friends.

It is during this adolescent stage that sixty percent or more of piano students drop out of music study. Actually our research indicates that only a very small percentage of these students ever resume their lessons. To the dropouts, their past music lessons represent a waste of time. Very few have mastered sufficient skills which could be used in later life. We have much empirical evidence that adults regret the fact that they did not continue their music lessons which they started as children. We have often heard the statement: "Why did my folks allow me to stop my music lessons?" Though upon reflection, they are usually at a loss to know how their folks could have controlled the situation at that time.

It is the policy of most teachers, parents and others having to do with children's guidance, to permit the discontinuance of the lessons under such circumstances. To quote one teacher: "You can't force such students to continue lessons or to love music or the piano. In addition, by not pressing the issue, there is always the chance they will return to music study at some future date."

The first three points are true enough, the last one is a grasp for straws since students rarely return to music without motivation.

However, there are institutions and individual

teachers who have taken the opposite view. For example, at the Harbor Conservatory we do press the issue, urging the child to go on with music lessons. We are convinced that the student innately loves music and does not realize how much he (or she) will miss the ability to make music in later years. Furthermore, if his lessons are uninterrupted until he is sixteen or seventeen, as we shall see in the next chapter, he will mature musically and will wish to study of his own volition. For these reasons, we are convinced it is our responsibility to use our influence to encourage the continuance of music lessons at this time.

How do we go about convincing the child to continue music lessons in spite of his strong feeling for quitting? First, we arrange heart to heart talks with the child. We listen with keen interest to the youngster's side of the story, *always recognizing his feelings as important factors to consider.* It is not difficult to get him to see how much he loves music, his kind of music. His attitude toward practicing is discussed as a normal, natural tendency, and it receives our acceptance and respect. Secondly, we present to him several alternatives to dropping music since that would cost him his ability to make the music that he loves so intensely. The options we present are as follows: he could go on with his lessons with the understanding that practicing would *not* be a required condition, i.e., he could practice if and when he pleased. If he wished, the material would be entirely of his own choosing. He could change teachers if he felt that a new personality would make his lessons more interesting. Lastly, he could change to another instrument such as the guitar.

With the alternatives presented in this way, it is not surprising to note the relatively large number of youngsters who elect to go on with their music. Some teachers and parents would argue that allowing a child to take piano lessons without practicing would constitute a waste of money and time spent on lessons because there could be no progress. *We can state without reservation that our experience has proven otherwise.* We have found that even when students did not practice at all between lessons *for one or two* years, there was reading and technical growth by virtue of the piano lessons alone. In short, there was some improvement in several skills. Of course, we concede such improvement could not be compared to that of students who did practice consistently. Nevertheless, the important factor to be considered is that when these youngsters awaken to their musical aspirations (at sixteen and seventeen), they are usually ready to practice and thus make up for their adolescent slack. Consequently, the parent and teacher must weigh for themselves the wisdom of permitting this slack period, keeping in mind the child's good chance of musical awakening later on, versus permitting him to quit his lessons—a decision which would most certainly bring about the end of music making for him.

A small percentage of students decide to change teachers with the hope that such a move will bring about a new enthusiasm. This sometimes proves effective if the personalities of student and teacher strike a harmonic chord between them. However, after an initial enthusiastic period, the student usually reverts to resistance to practicing. If this occurs, at this point no issue is made of it at the Harbor Conservatory.

Finally, a large percentage of the students elect to change from the piano to another instrument. This is usually to the guitar. The latter decision has its merits. It is a change to a "now" popular instrument, since many of their singing idols accompany themselves on the guitar and also many of their friends play it. As a result, there is motivation to learn the new instrument because there is the promise of immediate enjoyment due to peer approval. For many of the youngsters the interest in guitar is short lived, for they usually choose to return to piano lessons within a year or two. Of course, the final choice of instrument is not important since either one will further their music-making skills and give them the pleasure of expressing themselves throughout their lives. What is most important is that each student has the opportunity to explore different instruments and finally choose the one through which he feels he can best express himself.

Once the student has made his decision, we pursue it by convincing the parent to abide by the student's desire and to cooperate with our approach. Usually this request presents no problem. Most parents do not like the idea of the "easy solution", i.e., discontinuance of the lessons. So they agree to give their full cooperation, understanding that this is no easy task!

In sum, the adolescent stage is one of turbulence and resistance. It is the "I want to quit stage". This despite the fact that the teenager loves music more than even before. We believe it to be the responsibility of both parent and teacher to find ways to keep the student *at least* taking lessons until he has passed through this troublesome period into the more productive sixteen-seventeen year stage.

TEACHING PROCEDURES

Introduce keyboard harmony (Circle of Fifths and related chords) in preparation for jazz improvisation, and continue on to improvising (drill at lessons, do not expect results from home practicing).

Much sightreading—including jazz material.

Barbara January finds it beneficial at times to have two teenagers take their lessons at the same time, playing duets, sightreading together (in unison!) and improvising together (even freely).

11
Lisa
at Sixteen-Seventeen

WE NOW COME TO THE PERIOD in Lisa's musical life which makes all of the "growing pains" stages of her musical growth worth while. During her adolescence, Lisa, with her parents' consent, had elected to continue with her piano lessons with the condition that she could "practice if and when you wish and choose your own material". During that period, she practiced very little and most of each lesson was spent in sight-reading her choice of a rock or folk song, playing duets with the teacher, and learning about jazz and the basics for improvisation. It was an extremely hard time for the parent. In spite of the decision to continue with the lessons under such permissive conditions, the parent still had to deal with a resistant, argumentative Lisa. Furthermore, each lesson appeared to be "wasted", inasmuch as there was little or no practicing between lessons. Often, the parent was tempted to give up the entire project, but having gone along so far decided to "suffer" a little longer and see it through. The teacher also found it difficult. She found the lessons less than inspiring when week after week the student came with unprepared assignments. In addition, she had to deal with a Lisa who was only partially cooperative and was many times moody and sensitive.

However, now at Sixteen-Seventeen, Lisa has begun to change. She is becoming more confident of herself as an adult. As a junior-senior in high school she carries herself with a maturity expected of one who is in the upper classes. She is more discriminating in her choice of friends, and judges her peer values with greater care.

While she still is quite critical of her surrounding society and is determined to change it partially or drastically or even to "escape" from it entirely, she is less confused and intense about it than she was just a year ago. There are many things she now accepts which she had previously resisted. For example, the "authority" of teachers, officials, and sometimes even parents, is no longer the overriding issue it used to be. She accepts her responsibilities in certain areas, though she decides which areas they shall be. All in all, a more clearly defined personality has taken root, projecting a new awareness and social consciousness.

In music, the change is especially apparent. Lisa has begun to react to music with an intensity reminiscent of her six-seven year old period. While her adolescent reactions to music were strong and positive, they were quite limited in range. At that time, the words of the song were to her the important stimulation, expressing as they did inner feelings and emotions. The rhythm was equally important, giving release to pent-up inner conflicts and confusion. However, at Sixteen-Seventeen the music range had broadened. Yes, Lisa still sings and listens to rock and folk songs; the words and rhythm still have special meaning for her, but now the melodies and harmonies also attract her. This opens a new world for Lisa. Other kinds of music suddenly become meaningful. Lisa even finds some classical music awakens surprisingly lovely feelings.

Even more significant is the change in Lisa's attitude toward learning. She has become aware that she wants to play more proficiently. She recognizes that, to attain this, she must concentrate and work. Thus one finds her better organized in her practice and that she works with a determination to master assignments. Both parent and teacher find Lisa a pleasure these days in that she is completely self-motivated. Of course, she does not have as much time to devote to music as she would like. With homework and a full social life, Lisa must squeeze her practice time into spare time. Yet in spite of these limited hours of practicing, she makes significant progress. Her skills are developing. Most important of all she loves to make music, with the possibility that she will carry this capability with her all of her life.

We have come to the end of the saga of our composite typical character we have invented and named Lisa. Of course, Lisa does not represent all children at each of the age levels described in the last six chapters. There were varying percent-

GROWING PAINS IN NATURE'S MUSIC SCHEDULE*

Each child is different and will react to nature's music schedule in his own way. In general, however, a large percentage of children tend to follow the patterns depicted below.

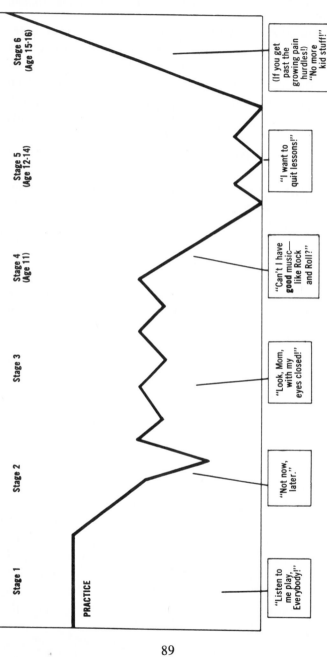

*Developmental graph. Reprinted from pamphlet: THIS BUSINESS OF MUSIC PRACTICING, or, How Six Words Prevented A Dropout, by Sidney J. Lawrence. 1968, Workshop Music Teaching Pub., Hewlett, N.Y.

ages of students at each stage whose reactions were different, and sometimes even the opposite, from those portrayed. For example, during the nine-ten year old stage, approximately twenty-five percent of the students did *not* play as fast as possible. These students *were* concerned with correct notes, rhythm and fingering. Another example is the adolescent years. Thirty-five percent had no wish to quit their lessons; fifty percent were not hostile or resistant, and approximately forty percent loved their music and music lessons.

Nevertheless, the evidence is that the majority of students are going to follow the path described in the preceding pages. The author is convinced that parent and teacher awareness of the year by year developmental patterns and their accompanying "growing pains" will lead to teacher and parent preparation for those events, and this should result in a considerable cut down of the number of "dropout" candidates.

PART III

The Individual Child

While it is true, as we have seen in the preceding chapters, that children at each age level tend to follow distinctive learning and behavioral patterns, it is equally true that regardless of age, each child's learning and behavioral style is different from those of other children. Each child comes to his first lesson with a certain level of confidence in his ability to learn, which may range from very high to a bottomless low. Each child sees teachers from a different perspective. Each child has already developed certain learning strengths and weaknesses. In the child's life up to the point of beginning lessons there has been established a basis for postures, attitudes, levels of aggressiveness or defensiveness as well as many other factors, all of which shape learning habits and behavior. We can project children's behavioral and learning changes at each age level but we must not lose sight of their individual differences. Our aim in this section of the book is to explore and discuss some of these differences.

12
Position in the Family

NOT LONG AFTER ALLEN'S LESSONS have begun, the teacher notices that Allen's chief interest in playing the piano is to finish as many pieces as he can in the shortest possible span of time. He greets each new piece and especially each new book with a cry of triumph. He is quite impatient with working through assignments at the lesson, and simply refuses to repeat assignments the second week, even though the repetition may be necessary to learn something new, to improve a skill, or to correct a fault. He seems compelled to plunge forward. Allen seems to be competing with someone; it becomes apparent after a while that the rival is Allen's younger brother.

On the other hand, Allen's younger brother, Ben, spends his lesson time in a constant state of anxiety. He makes a minimum effort. He gives up at the first attempt. He seems to be saying, "I can't win this contest with my brother, so I'll pretend that I don't care if I lose". At this point the teacher correctly suspects Ben has been "behind" his brother most of the time because he is resigned to accepting the role of "the loser".

Of course, in other instances where the teacher has siblings as students, the roles may be reversed. It may be the younger child who is aggressive and the older one who has given up.

To explain the effects of family constellation in more detail: the birth-order position in the family is one of the important factors influencing the direction of the child's attitude toward learning and his behavior in a learning situation. Alfred Adler discovered that among siblings, there is a constant struggle for recognition and power. The nature of the recognition and power sought depends upon the birth-order position in the family and this factor influences the basic foundation of one's life style. Talent and ability are greatly affected. Sometimes the struggle for power may tend to build certain characteristics to maximum strength. In other situations, talent may be dulled or negated. Ability may be handicapped or impaired or skills may develop sluggishly. Adler has pointed out "the very position of the child in the family may lend shape and colour to all the instincts, tropisms, faculties and the like which he brings with him to the world. This affirmation robs of all value the theories of the inheritness of special traits or talents, which are so harmful to the educational effort."[1] Lucille Forer com-

---

[1] Alfred Adler, Understanding Human Nature; N.Y. Greenberg, Pub., 1927. 1946.

ments: "Researchers have found that there are specific strengths and weaknesses, inherent in each birth-order position."[2]

Thus we learn that each position in the family has its own special qualities, sometimes strong and positive and sometimes quite weak and harmful. Following is a list of common characteristics in students stemming from the Birth-Order Factor:

First Born: Conscientious, achieves well. Often is over-anxious and tense—appears to be looking continuously over his shoulder to see if his younger sibling is catching up. Sometimes gives up easily after first failure. Easily frustrated.

Second Born: Adaptive, learns well. Often appears to be expending much energy trying to catch up to older sibling. Usually has more confidence than the older sibling, unless he feels overwhelmed and then he also gives up easily.

Middle Child: Placid, phlegmatic, tends to learn more slowly. Makes the teacher "come to him", while he himself expends little energy in responding. Gives the impression of trying half-heartedly to catch up to older sibling, while at the same time looks fearfully behind him to see whether the younger sibling is catching up. However, his end-result is often surprisingly better than the others.

Youngest Child: Some act like they are determined to "excel every member of the family" to

[2]Lucille Forer, with Henry Still, The Birth Order Factor; New York, David McKay, 1976.

use Adler's words.[3] Others lack self-confidence, are sometimes intimidated by the older siblings and frequently shy away from concentration at lessons and practice at home.

Only Child: Some are over-mature (too grown-up in manners), and will try hard, but are anxious and uncertain about task-fulfillment. "There may be an internal dependency conflict".[4] "He is frequently harried by the thought he cannot possibly live up to the expectations his parents hold for him."[5]

Obviously, these attitudes which the children bring with them to their music lessons are going to be important factors in colouring their musical aims and in determining how much and how effectively they will learn. For example, Allen's musical aims are distorted and sidetracked by his inner unconscious drive to outdo his brother. Allen's brother, Ben, has also distorted his musical aims by his defensiveness and role as the "defeated" one. An only child might be playing very well but for the wrong reasons. His sole musical aim could be to please his parents (or the teacher). As can be seen, the life styles and attitudes affected by the birth-order tend to hinder and sidetrack both the development of musical skills, and the sheer enjoyment of music.

It will serve the end-result well if the teacher will study the child and determine what motivates his drive and behavior. Is he so ambitious because

---

[3]Adler, ibid.
[4]Forer, ibid.,
[5]Lawrence, ibid.

he is the youngest child and must prove that he is best in the family? Or does he give up easily because he is an only child and is accustomed to having everything done for him? The questions could go on and on!

The teacher's conclusions may suggest a change in prognosis as to end-results. He may well estimate that the level of skill-mastery and, more important, the capacity for musical response could turn out to be lower than otherwise might have been expected. In some cases he might even foresee premature dropouts. In general he must anticipate that the family constellation struggle will in some measure create a background conducive to early "quitting".

Can the piano teacher do anything about this? Can he alter the child's life style to the extent of sublimating musical aims and work-drive into more self-serving directions?

The answer is yes. In the first place, sensitive piano teachers often instinctively use their influence to motivate and inspire the child. Here the teacher needs to go but one step further. In all contacts with students, the teacher must subtly impress the child that his music-making is solely the "property" of the child, belonging to him alone. It is not to be "loaned" or "given away" in the form of a "contest" with his brother, or as a "present" to please his mother or father, or even as a "bribe" to win the teacher's approval. He is learning to play for himself, his *most* important audience. He is learning to play for *his* personal pleasure, first, and for others' enjoyment only if *he* so desires. It does not matter whether he plays better than anyone else in the world. What matters is that *he* can express *his* musical feelings on the piano. It is perfectly acceptable for him to learn at his *own* pace, slow or fast, without regard to how fast or slow anyone else is learning.

When the child is convinced that all of this is actually what is expected of him, he is generally much relieved and his chances of continuing his music education are greatly improved.

In addition, the information the teacher has gathered about the child's motivation aids him in more immediate practical ways. His approach, his tone of voice, his choice of goals and his selection of assignments from lesson to lesson will be geared to help the child build confidence and a sense of self-worth. Depending on the teacher's plan of action, his approach may be verbal and explanatory, or it may be silent; it may utilize demonstration or student exploration. The teacher's voice-tone may be persuasive, demanding, firm, loving, humorous, or matter-of-fact, depending upon whether stimulation, firm guidance, reasurance, etc., is desired. As goals, the teacher may, for example, choose reading skills to build self-confidence, or memorizing a little piece for a sense of personal accomplishment. He will select assignments best calculated to bring about a feeling of personal pleasure and a sense of continual progress in playing.

In sum, the birth-order factor is a force to be reckoned with in music learning and in the question of musical dropouts. Add it to the year by year learning and behavioral patterns in music training and we see one more aspect in the overview of the piano student.

13

Differences in Learning Styles

THERE IS ANOTHER ASPECT in the makeup of piano students which makes for differences among them and which affects the teaching approach. We refer to the means by which each student learns.

Every teacher has dealt with the following types of student: the child who plays everything by ear but finds reading difficult; the child who sightreads everything in front of him but cannot play from memory; and the child who plays everything by finger position or a sense of touch, but cannot read or pick out a tune.

Such children are typical. They exemplify an important fact: we learn music by utilizing three of our senses. To play the piano we use eyes, ears and touch. Each of these senses respond to its own perception, its own retention and its own reflex conditioning. We use them all in the learning processes of making music. The professional musician is well trained in using all three senses equally well. The average, normal student tends to lean on or emphasize one of the three over the others. Annie J. Curwin long ago categorized the student as being either a Visual, Audile or Tactile.[1]

Tommy plays by ear. What does this really mean? Not only does Tommy have a mental image of how the song sounds, but he can picture the spacing, going up or down or remaining on the same pitch, of each tone as related to the last one. He has a clear inner picture as to how the rhythm goes, he can hear the pulse, etc. All he has to do is find the equivalent keys on the piano —if he has good auditory-hand coordination, he can play the melody of the song as soon as he hears it, much to the admiration of those around him. It is probable that Tommy learns everything else by ear also. When he is instructed verbally as compared to learning from a blackboard, or from reading the text, he may absorb the information much more quickly and solidly. For this reason he cannot read music very well. Indeed, he is so slow at it, it frustrates him and he avoids reading as much as possible. In his case, his visual imagery, visual memory and eye-hand coordination are more sluggish than his hearing. One cannot blame Tommy for favoring his most effective sense to make music.

---

[1]Mrs. Spencer J. Curwin, Psychology Applied To Music Teaching, London, J. Curwin & Sons, Schirmer, 1900.

Jane is a fine sightreader. Her eyes sweep over several measures of notes, taking in all of them in the one glance with a fair degree of accuracy. Hardly looking at the piano, she moves her hands and fingers over the corresponding keys. Her visual perception is sharp enough, its retention is strong enough, and her eye-hand coordination is quick enough for her to set her hands and fingers *without consciously thinking about it* into the proper position to play the indicated keys in the required rhythm. She hardly ever looks at the keyboard, for it is registered in her mind like a photograph. However, Jane cannot play by ear, and she finds improvising quite complicated. The truth is she does not *hear* what she sightreads. To her, tones are rather hazy; she cannot pick out tunes. Chord sounds are beyond her. In her case, is it possible that, in school, she does not do as well with verbal instruction, as she might with written work, exams and a textbook?

Michael sounds very impressive at the piano. He has facility, can play fast scale and arpeggio passages and in general exhibits much technical skill. Michael is a Tactile, i.e., his strongest sense is his sense of touch. He easily retains a mental picture of what he has touched, of the feeling of the amount of space between fingers, and of which fingers he uses. Once he has played something (usually by rote or via laborious reading of note by note) his fingers have "memorized" it, and he can play it at double the speed required. However, Michael can neither read music nor hear it. It is likely that Michael has trouble learning in school.

However, it is possible if he were taught through kinesthetic or tactile means he could find learning easier and more interesting.

The three examples, of course, are extremes. Most children do make use of all three senses even though they tend to depend on one more than on the others. However, the degree of dependency on a selected sense will vary from one student to another. Thus each student requires a special teaching approach which fits his particular strengths and weaknesses.

The student who relies confidently on his eye-hand coordination is best equipped, usually, for he develops well in reading skills. According to the Carryover Report, children who learn to read adequately rarely drop out of music study.

However, the student who learns mainly "by ear" will at one time or another, develop music learning problems, and unfortunately, the child who leans heavily on his tactile sense is likely to develop the severest problems of all. As a matter of fact, the Audile and the Tactile will develop problems which, if left unattended, lead to frustration, discouragement and often finally to a decision to quit music training altogether.

At first, in the latter instances, the problem for the teacher is that he himself might so easily be misled by the seemingly rapid progress at the lessons. Afterwards, when he is aware that the progress has been an illusion, the larger problem is attempting to backtrack and rebuild a sound sense-learning balance.

Here is a typical example: Michael, playing almost entirely through his tactile sense, impresses everyone with his accurate facility on the keyboard. Even his teacher, who is not yet aware that he has been "faking" his reading, is impressed and is lavish with praise. Michael seems to be playing at a very advanced level for the short time he has been studying. One can understand Michael's pride in himself because, on the surface, it appears that he is developing much faster with his music than his friends are. However, the moment of reckoning arrives when the pieces get more difficult. In order to play the up-graded music he must first read it correctly. Since his music reading is so weak; since the pieces become more complicated in notation and rhythm, he must labor more and more on simply deciphering what is contained on the staff. This often proves to be too much for him. Rather than give the required attention, energy, and concentration needed to overcome the reading weakness, Michael eliminates the problem by deciding to discontinue his lessons. This is the course most youngsters like Michael tend to follow.

The teacher can do much to counteract and insulate against this type of learning problem. From the beginning special attention should be placed on the development and coordination of *all* three senses with the hands. A continual check should be made to see that none of the senses are being even partially neglected. However, since quick visual note recognition and eye-hand coordination are the most important—and the most overlooked—of the three areas, children do need additional emphasis here to insure competence.

For this reason, the teacher must always be

on the alert to see that the learning of notation *is* being absorbed from the *very beginning*. The same holds true for the geography of the keyboard. There needs to be eye-hand drills at every lesson during the early months, reviewed again and again, even though the child appears to be learning his notes well. Rapid recognition of notation is a basic goal. A second goal is finding the equivalent keys, which also must be done rapidly, with eyes fastened on the music book as much as possible. When there is resistance from the student, the sensitive teacher will alternate the tedious drills with familiar tunes played by ear, which should minimize the resistance. Only when the child equalizes his reading ability with his "ear" and/or touch playing can the teacher feel that the child is ready for normal development in music.

Many such students come from other teachers, sometimes after years of training. The former teachers were often unaware of the student's reading problems, simply identifying the children as poor music students. Since the students had never learned to read music, they depended completely on their ear-playing or tactile sense. The fact that they were ready to try another teacher is a very encouraging indication. The new teacher can make good use of the "fresh" relationship; he is in an advantageous position to impress upon the student the importance of learning to read music, and therefore the necessity to learn notation from the very beginning. In most instances, the student willingly complies with a new teacher under these circumstances.

It should be noted at this point that many of

the "ear" players who drop out of music training continue playing without further lessons. They teach themselves, by ear of course. They sometimes play quite well, and a large percentage of them continue to play throughout their adult life (See Appendix). Very few learn how to read music, however. I have never met one of these self-taught musicians who did not deeply regret his inability to read music.

In sum, the third aspect in the overview or profile of the piano student is his learning style—the sense by which he learns. Whichever learning sense he favors, the remaining ones tend to become proportionately weaker and thus may affect his general musical growth.

14
Potential Problems

A COLLEAGUE OF MINE once enumerated the many problems she found among her students:

Alice had visual problems. She had been cross-eyed and while she had had a series of operations which had "straightened" her eyes cosmetically, she still saw through only one eye, and had a problem recognizing her notes.

Stanley had a slight hearing impairment in one ear, and often missed what was being said.

John was overactive. He was continually moving about, diverting his attention, being loud and playful. His teacher found it difficult to instruct him.

Joanne was slow. Everything had to be repeated over and over again until she comprehended it.

Melinda was overanxious. She was always highly tense at the lesson and this caused her to overlook a great deal that was being taught to her.

Bruce was hostile. He vibrated anger at the

lesson, and the teacher found it difficult to get through to him.

Agnes tried too hard to please. She seemed to live for her teacher's approval.

We could go on and on. One could easily conclude, and probably be not too far from the truth, that every music student has some sort of problem. Some of these problems, without doubt, stem from normal growth development, as in Lisa's case. Others may be reflections of the Birth-Order Factor. There are those who have the learning problems discussed in the last chapter, while there are still others as in the above, who are affected by physical or psychological difficulties. The point is that all of these problems, in one way or another, influence the student's efficiency in learning, his capability for self-discipline, as well as his stamina. Since most children are vulnerable, potential "common problems" must be considered a vital factor when we examine the overview of the whole student. It is our fourth and final factor.

The solution to each of these problems will depend upon the teacher's own method, personality and initiative. Often the awareness of the problem by itself dictates the solution. For example, the teacher dealt with Alice's visual impairment by assigning method books with large notation. The instructor offset Stanley's hearing difficulty by speaking more distinctly and always facing him as he spoke. With John, the overactive, the teacher patiently, sympathetically, but firmly insisted that he sit at the lesson and pay strict attention to his teacher. Concurrently, she invented games, challenges, races, stories, etc., to draw and hold his attention.

The most important factor is the *awareness* of the existence of a problem. Too often, the teacher simply fails to see that there is a difficulty or misinterprets the situation. Such errors of omission and commission may contribute to the student's frustration and discouragement and simply lead to one more dropout. For example, the above mentioned colleague related with much chagrin how she had overlooked Melinda's anxiety. Instead of seeing a child who needed reassurance, approval and ego build-up, the teacher scolded her for lack of preparation, without further investigation. It was not until the child dropped out that the teacher realized how wrong her approach had been.

In the case of Agnes, also, the teacher at first did not see the actual problem. Agnes was the student who played only for approval. The teacher, during the initial period, heaped praise on the child for her well prepared assignments. Fortunately, she soon began to notice that Agnes' reactions were rather extreme. For example, the child's face glowed with delight when the teacher said something kind, or she would hold back the tears if the teacher, concentrating on items to be corrected, neglected to mention she had played nicely. Now that the teacher understood the direction of Agnes' needs, she changed her approach. To redirect the child's dependency on adult approval, the teacher launched on a campaign aimed at building a feeling of self-worth within the child, so that she could derive her own inner satisfaction from her piano playing. It was emphasized continually that the teacher was simply the vehicle, albeit a very friendly one, to bring about improved playing skills. In time, this approach proved itself and Agnes learned to play very well, indeed, becoming quite happy with her music.

Awareness of the problem is seventy-five percent of the battle. The other twenty-five percent is dealing with it. The piano teacher, today, is more psychologically oriented than ever before. In most instances he will instinctively and intuitively find the best solution.

There is another type of learning problem, not mentioned above, which is difficult to diagnose and even more difficult to correct. I refer to "perceptual difficulties".

Unfortunately, this type of problem appears to be widespread, encompassing anywhere from twenty-five to thirty-five percent of music students (this estimate is based on an empirical survey we made some years ago at the Harbor Conservatory. We *do* know without question that a large percentage of children who come to us show symptoms of this type of problem).

Perceptual difficulties are a minor form of the impediment known today in such various terms as "perceptual impairment", "perceptual disability", or "perceptual dysfunction". These describe a more serious malady categorized generally as Minimal-Brain-Damaged, and usually requires the aid of an educational specialist. Those teachers interested in knowing more about perceptual impairment, etc., in relationship to one-to-one piano teaching, are referred to CHALLENGES IN MU-

SIC TEACHING.[1] In this chapter, perceptual *difficulties*, less severe than the above, refers to children whose eyesight and hearing are generally normal and who are capable of dealing with most of their school subjects on a passing basis. However, they have various degrees of difficulty with reading, or understanding clearly what is being said. They apparently have the same problems with their music, they have trouble recognizing notation and coordinating eyes and hands.

The child with perceptual difficulties has some problems with depth perception. In his mind, he cannot easily separate the staff lines in order to decide quickly on which line or space the note is on. The same applies to the keyboard. He sees an endless number of white keys and he finds it quite a task to organize them so that he can play properly.

Such children should not be grouped with students who are merely confused in music reading. The latter have difficulties usually because their perception is *too* sharp, *too* clear. They tend sometimes to see minute differences of note shapes and stem lengths even in engraved music on the printed page and tend to become confused by them. Because of the sharpness of their perception they often have optical illusions of note position on the staff, thus adding to their confusion.[2]

The teacher can easily check to determine

---

[1]Sidney J. Lawrence; CHALLENGES IN PIANO TEACH-ING, Hewlett, N.Y., Workshop Music Teaching Pub. 1978.

[2]See REMEDIAL SIGHTREADING FOR THE PIANO STUDENT, ibid.

whether the child is a possible "perceptual" case. Does he know his right hand from his left? After seven years of age, this should be no problem. Which is his dominant hand? Is it the correct one for him? It is said that the use of the wrong hand can cause perceptual problems.[3] This is based on the fact that the right side of the brain controls the left side of the body, and vice versa. To determine the dominant side, observe which foot he uses when he starts walking, and/or have him make a telescope with his hands and look at some object. The eye he uses will be his dominant one, and that side of his body should be dominant. Where the child uses the opposite hand for writing this is called "cross-dominance". However, more than half of the students we have tested who turn out cross-dominant, have no trouble reading in school or learning to read music. Therefore, it should not be assumed if the child is cross-dominant that he will automatically have perceptual difficulties. These tests merely indicate potential vulnerability, and could help us determine the possible type of problem we may be dealing with.

A further little test, more trustworthy than the question of handedness, is asking the child to recite the alphabet in reverse starting from *G*. Of course, the child should be at least eight years old. Children who have slight perceptual problems will labor, make many errors, but will finally succeed in this recitation. If unsuccessful, he may

---

[3]See Sutphin, A PERCEPTUAL TRAINING AND HANDBOOK, 1964, Winterhaven Lion Research.

have a severe perceptual problem and should be referred to any institution which specializes in this area.[4]

Even when it is only a minor case of perceptual difficulty, the teacher must be prepared for a long, tedious patient effort. To begin with, the musical foundation must be made as solid as possible. Each step of music training should begin with drills emphasizing pitch direction and rhythm division away from the piano, then singing with the hand moving in the same direction as the tones. It is often best to introduce notation with the Orff approach—first just a one line staff, with one note on it, one note below it and one note above it. Then introduce another line and note, etc. All of this should be introduced step by step, and no new step undertaken until the student has understood the last one. This procedure should be carried out until the child is completely familiar with notes and rhythm. Only then will he be ready to go to the keyboard. A similar approach should be used on the keyboard, one note at a time.

In sum, the various problems listed in this chapter are common to "normal" children and must be considered a factor in their musical development. Failure to recognize and deal with the problem contributes to early dropouts. By understanding them the skillful and sympathetic teacher can guide the student to ultimate mastery of music-making skills.

---

[4]Ibid. CHALLENGES.

PART IV

Steps Toward Carryover

With the overview completed, the teacher is faced with the following considerations. How can he better evaluate his student in view of the information contained in these pages? How can he best educate the parent of the student in an understanding of the child with a view to the best approach to musical goals? How does the teacher-student relationship affect the training? What else can the teacher do to assure carryover?

In the final chapters of this book we will address ourselves to these questions.

15

The Initial Interview—
Profile of the Student

EACH CHILD BRINGS TO HIS INITIAL IN-
TERVIEW the sum total of his life's experience.
As has been stated in earlier chapters, his personality has begun to take shape and so have his
attitudes toward adults, teachers, education and,
of course, music. He brings with him learning
habits which are still being shaped. He has developed strengths and weaknesses. He is at a
specific stage of development and is responding in
a typical fashion (more or less) for his age. His
outlook is already strongly coloured by his position
in his family, he is on the way to establishing a
favored learning sense, and may have developed
problems in one or two areas.

The initial interview can be used effectively
as a vehicle to gather preliminary information
about the student before lessons begin. Even a
small amount of insight gained by carefully
planned questions and simple tests could help set

more practical, attainable goals as well as the tone of the teaching approach, and in the end, the teacher could use such knowledge to develop an individualized teaching program to fit the student's particular personality and learning patterns.

Obviously, the primary objective is to obtain the clearest overall profile possible of the student in order to determine his physical and musical strengths and weaknesses. Another important objective would be to check for possible future problems so that they might be immediately confronted with possible methods of solution. As to the latter point, some may ask, why not wait for the problem to appear and then set about correcting it. Admittedly, sometimes this is a preferable approach, but in most instances if the pattern is deeply established, its solution is doubly difficult. Whenever feasible, it is wiser to work at prevention than on a cure.

The following pages describe the Harbor Conservatory approach to testing at the initial interview. In general, our interviews have resulted in decided improvements in individual teaching plans, selection of materials, determination of student's pace of development, and progress expectancy. Although there have been occasional errors in evaluating the student, this never turned out to be detrimental to him—it is less harmful to deal with a problem and find there isn't one, than to assume normality and later on discover the problem.

The aims of the interview should be kept in mind as the tests are read: it is important to know the child's attitudes toward his environment, to learning in general, and to music in particular. His stage of learning development, learning style and attitude toward instruction are important characteristics to be determined. Is he mentally alert? Slow and sluggish? Are his hands and fingers adaptable? Will they need special attention at the piano? Does he have problems in the visual, perceptual, psychological categories? There are more questions the teacher will think of, and many of the answers may be forthcoming at the interview.

At the Harbor Conservatory the first part of the interview includes the questions noted above and are asked of both students and parents. The answers, and the manner in which they are answered, should be observed and recorded. Important also is the relationship between the child and parent, assuming this can be determined at the interview.

The following test is then given (some of these items were described in other chapters. They are given here, again, because now we are concerned with establishing normality):

Step 1. The child is asked to recite the alphabet through *G*. He is then asked to reverse it. This determines how far the child has progressed in his conceptual development. Most children have not developed reversability until they are seven or eight. And for understanding notation this is critical.

A child of seven or eight should respond slowly, with much thought between each answer. If he doesn't, he may be a late developer in this area and should wait a year or two for lessons. Nine should respond with less deliberation, and

Ten and older should respond quite quickly. If children of this age are unable to reverse mentally they are not ready for regular piano lessons. They may be late developers or have some learning disability.

Step 2. At the piano the student echoes rhythm phrases played by the teacher. The teacher plays the patterns on high *C* only. The student attempts to repeat the same patterns on Middle *C.* After the teacher plays a single phrase, the student imitates it. We use the following sequences: *(1)* | | | *(2)* | ⊓ | *(3)* | | ⊓ | *(4)* | | | ⊓ | *(5)* | | | | ⊓ | etc. Note that each group utilizes eighth notes one beat later than the last group. Most seven and eight year old children usually respond correctly to (1) (2) (3). The eight year old generally adds (4) correctly. Nine year olds the same. Over ten should add (5) and up. If the child's tempo is an exact replica of the teacher's (especially six, seven and eight year olds) rhythmic hearing superiority and exceptional motor control is indicated. If the beat is sluggish, but the time values reasonably right, this might show an acceptable rhythmic "ear", but slower motor control. The seven year old who responds well to (4) or (5) definitely indicates superior rhythmic hearing as well as higher development in motor control. If he achieves only (1) or (2) we must feel he has either a poor sense of rhythm and/or motor control, or he is behind in his development. Similarly eight and nines who can respond correctly after (4) are rated superior, while those below (4) are considered lower than average.

Step 3. The student plays five notes on the piano in diatonic sequence, using the five fingers of his right hand. He then repeats with his left hand. The control of each finger is noted. The teacher observes whether the fingers are tense or jelly-like, the knuckles firm or collapsing, the joints strong or loose. Does he press with his body when he presses a finger? Does he exert so little energy that his fingers cannot press the keys down? These tests could indicate whether the child is anxious, shy, has little confidence, is impatient, easily frustrated, or, on the other hand, is friendly, confident, eager and a potential avid learner.

Step 4. Other possible problems are now investigated. How does the student respond to general education? Does he read at peer level? What is his behavior record at home and at school? How is his eyesight and hearing? Test results may be available from public school records, or the parent may have medical information. Here we are considering the possible slow learner, the late learner, the hyperactive type, as well as the child who may have trouble seeing or hearing.

Additional problems, more complex, are then investigated. Are there possible perceptual or co-ordination problems? Both are far more common than we realize. For these the symptoms are confused reversed thinking as in step 1, difficulty in responding physically as in step 2. Another simple test is the telescope test described in the last chapter.

This, then, is the means whereby we obtain the beginnings of a profile of the student. Since one interview may be misleading, everything we have learned is subject to change. Nevertheless, we should be able to anticipate certain problems and minimize their growth as well as the ultimate damage they might otherwise cause.

The following is a sample profile sheet to be filled out for the teacher's confidential files:

STUDENT PROFILE

Name .... Address .... Tel. ....

Age .... Siblings (according to age) ....

HISTORY (from parent—child not present):

Eyesight normal ....glasses........................problems........................

Hearing normal ....impairment.....................................

School: good student .... above av. .... fair .... just passing...........

Reading: poor .... slow learner .... late learner .... good ....

Behavior problem .... other prob. in school .... at home ....

Does everything conscientiously .... well organized .... poorly org. ....

Does not do homework .... does homework under pressure .... how many

hours of tv per day? .... behavior prob. at home .... emotional prob. ....

Does child see a specialist? .... Should teacher know something special about

child? ....

....

HISTORY (from student, if he had previous musical training):

How long had he studied .... Names of previous teachers ....

....

Why did he stop with them ....

What kind of music does he like the most ....

What are his hobbies outside of music ....

TEACHER'S EVALUATION OF PLAYING:

Names of composition played ....

General appraisal ....

Strong points in playing ....

Weak points ....

EXAMINATION (Include beginners):

Reverse alphabet from *G*: fast...........normal...........slow...........gets conf............

is unable to do it....................

Perceptual: R.H./R.E.............L.H./L.E............R.H./L.E............L.H./R.E............

Learning style (first impression): Visual .... Audile .... Tactile ....

can't judge ....

Coordination: Ear-hand-rhythm test: (1) | | | .... (2) | ⊓ | ....

(3) | | ⊓ | .... (4) | | | ⊓ | .... (5) | | | | ⊓ | ....

(6) | | | | | ⊓ |............ (7) | | | | | | ⊓ |............

Finger independence—(five finger scale up and down): R.H. all fingers good

.... all fingers tense .... list ind. finger(s) which do not work ....

L.H.: all fingers good .... all fingers tense .... list ind. finger(s) which

do not work .... list weak joints .... limp fingers ....

TEACHER'S OBSERVATIONS: Child's att. to teacher ....

child's att. to parent ....

parent's att. to child (ex.: does she allow child to answer for himself)

....

The above is intended as a guide to help the teacher make up his own examination, utilizing his own experience and his own teaching principles. It is recommended that he use the above as a base, adding to it or subtracting from it to suit his own teaching circumstances.

16
Parental Re-Education

AS THE PIANO TEACHER KNOWS ONLY TOO WELL, parental support and cooperation are essential ingredients in achieving success in training a child to play the piano. One may put it more strongly. The mother and father have a definite responsibility, a role they must play which contributes to that success. When the parents do not fulfill that role, or do not understand their responsibility, or shirk it, all of the teacher's skill and efforts could well be in vain. While it has been done, it is a rare child who can learn to play the piano in spite of his parents.

Clearly, parental education is called for. In light of the erroneous handed-down notions as to how the child should respond to music lessons, obviously what is required is re-education. The parents, like the teacher, must divest themselves of that old scenario. They should be re-educated *in advance of lessons* in the new overview of the child, and more than this, they must be made aware of the importance of their own roles. and responsibilities. While the concepts described in these pages are new and often startling and sometimes even shocking to the majority of parents, they generally understand quickly and are usually eager to learn and do their share.

Most teachers hold regular parental meetings or occasional parental get-togethers during which they define for the parents their roles. Other teachers elect to meet individually with the parents for the same purpose. In any case, it must be stressed again that the new overview of the child, and the new role of the parent, should be presented as clearly as possible before lessons begin. These points should be repeated constantly over the years as the child develops. The repetition is especially necessary because parents, like teachers, sometimes revert to old patterns of thinking and behavior. Constant reminders are re-enforcing.

The following points should be stressed and discussed in some detail:

1. The parent should clearly understand that music-training is a six to eight year venture, the overall period of lessons depending upon many factors in the child's growth and development. Music training cannot depend on a "see whether he takes to it" basis anymore than can reading or arithmetic in the public school. Parents must see to it that the child also understands it this way.

2. Music training moves in spurts, or at a snail's pace, according to the child's developmental stage. Sometimes progress is apparent, sometimes there appears to be a plateau, sometimes there seems to be retrogression. Whenever learning and behavioral changes are taking place, the

odds are that they are normal and typical of the child's age level, and should not be the cause for dismay or disenchantment. When there is reason to suspect that the changes are not normal or typical, the teacher is the person to consult, not the child. Indeed, such matters should *never* be discussed in the child's presence unless there is carefully thought out reason for doing so.

3. There is a misconception of what constitutes "lack of interest" in music. The parent should understand that *every* child is *always* interested in music, only the *type* of music will vary and change. This is absolutely true even though he loudly proclaims that he "hates" music, or he practices less than enthusiastically, or doesn't practice at all. The parent may express astonishment at such a statement and may well ask, "If that is the case, why does my child act in this way?" The reason is simple. The child's protests and resistance are subconsciously meant to give his mother and/or father a message which is not related in any way to "interest in music". His real message may be one of several complaints. He may not yet be organized enough to know how to practice, which may frustrate him. Or practicing may be interfering with a preferred activity. Or else practicing may have become a confrontation of wills between parent and child in an ongoing parent-child conflict, and the child is using it essentially as a weapon in that struggle. Furthermore, there may be a learning problem which is discouraging the student (in which case, of course, the teacher should be contacted), and finally and more frequently, his message is merely an empty gesture typical of a particular stage in

the child's normal behavioral growth in music training.

In any case, the parent should never discontinue piano lessons on the ground of a "lack of interest" any more than he or she would discontinue the child's training in reading and writing in school for such reasons.

4. Finally, it is the parent's responsibility to help the child develop normally and naturally in his musical growth, through all of his ups and downs, through problem periods as well as inspired periods. For this reason, the parent must, like the teacher, learn to anticipate the changes likely to take place from year to year and to prepare to deal with them in the most positive, effective way possible. The mother and father will always be wary of impulses to discontinue lessons when there is a drop or lull in the child's progress or attitude toward practicing.

In addition to the verbal re-education of the parent, the teacher should make up a list of parental "do's" and "don'ts". He will find this an effective re-enforcement. Some teachers buy and hand out to the parents copies of THIS BUSINESS OF MUSIC PRACTICING, or HOW SIX WORDS PREVENTED A DROPOUT, a pamphlet designed to give the information discussed above in story form.[1]

Here is a sample of "do's" and "don'ts" reprinted from that pamphlet:

---

[1]For Information regarding the purchase of copies write WORKSHOP MUSIC TEACHING PUB. 315 Mill Road. Hewlett, N.Y. 11557

"Do's" for Parents[1]:

TEN WAYS TO HELP YOUR CHILD IN NATURE'S MUSIC SCHEDULE

1. Make clear to your child at the very outset of lessons — in manner enthusiastic, of course — that music training is a long term program — just as schooling is. And that there are many high points of pleasure along the way.

2. Your child has his own pace to follow, so avoid comparing him with siblings or neighbor's children who appear to be playing better than he. Anticipate "ups and downs" in his attitudes and practicing — and a number of "growing pain" periods, besides.

3. Make a study of how to help your child. Deciding when to help, when to be supportive and when to withdraw to the background permitting him to help himself, is a parental art in itself.

4. Remember to stress that the quality — not the quantity — of practicing is what counts for real progress.

5. "Music comes to the child more naturally when there is music in his mother's speaking voice," says the distinguished violin educator, Suzuki. So be pleasant and encouraging about your child's practicing. Of course there will be occasions when you will need to be firm. But remember — "music in your voice"—*teach* him, *guide* him, but don't *police* him!

6. When you help your child, be at his side — not at the other end of the room, or in the next room. Teach him to treat the practice session with the same respect he gives to his lesson period.

7. Don't despair if practicing becomes non-existent for a while, your child will make progress anyhow at the lesson itself—though it will be slower.

8. During a "crisis," always "talk it out" with your child on the basis of *mutual respect*. Be sure, if it's real serious, to discuss it with the teacher first. Allow your child a voice in the final. decision, though be sure it is a constructive one.

9. A sense of humor is a powerful weapon with which to dispel clashes over practicing.

10. Always let your child feel you are proud of his achievements, even if they are small.

---

[1]Reprinted from THIS BUSINESS OF MUSIC PRACTICING OR HOW SIX WORDS PREVENTED A DROPOUT, Workshop Music Teaching Pub. Hewlett, N.Y.

"Don'ts" for Parents[1]:

AVOID THESE TRAPS!

Don't ever belittle your child's efforts. Don't threaten to stop his lessons if he doesn't practice. This threat may work during periods of high interest in music, but it is likely to boomerang during a "growing pain" period. The day may come when he will remind you of it and insist that you make good your threat.

Don't criticize your child for "lack" of interest or poor or no practicing in the presence of others, especially his music teacher. The teacher has skillfully built up a fine relationship with your child, and "losing face" tends to undermine it. Speak to the teacher privately about problems, and to others not at all.

Your financial investment in your child's music lessons pays its dividends by the skills he acquires over the years, not by the amount of daily practicing he does, or how much he plays for company or even for you. Always remember you are giving your child a music education for *his* use and for *his* self expression and pleasure. Don't expect him to be "grateful" for your sacrifices in giving him music lessons; his gratitude will come years later when he can play and enjoy himself as an adult.

---

[1]Reprinted from THIS BUSINESS OF MUSIC PRACTICING OR HOW SIX WORDS PREVENTED A DROPOUT, Workshop Music Teaching Pub. Hewlett, N.Y.

17
The Teacher-Student Relationship

THE QUALITY OF THE RELATIONSHIP BE-
TWEEN the teacher and the student remains to
be discussed. The dedicated teacher is much aware
of the meaning of such relationships. Its importance cannot be overemphasized for often it has
a lifetime effect. A strong rapport will lessen the
difficulty the teacher has in getting through the
rough spots, and an atmosphere conducive to
stronger work motivation will heighten and inspire
the student to loftier levels of music-making. Whatever the results, they are felt for years to come
in terms of habits and impressions formed and
memories of the teacher and their relationship.

In speaking to adult amateur musicians, we
often hear of the effects of their teacher relationship, "Ah, if it were not for Mrs. X, my piano
teacher, I would not be playing today! I loved
her!" "My teacher was genuinely interested in
me. She cared not only about my music, but me

as a person!" I have even heard the remark: "I cared as much for my music teacher as my own mother!" The teacher's influence on his student can be one of the most far reaching in the student's life.

The basic element in a successful teacher-student relationship is trust. When the student fully trusts the teacher's feelings he will respond by dissolving a good part of his anxiety, tension, defensiveness and the need to divert from the tasks at hand. If he is convinced the teacher understands and likes him, does not form moral judgments or disapprove of him, is correcting his musical errors in order to truly *help* him to make music, not to show how "stupid" he is, then he is more likely to progress naturally and happily at his lessons. Of course there will be problems. Of course the student will move faster or slower or not at all as his particular stage of development dictates. However, there will be a heightening of the level of motivation during the best time, just as there is a marked lowering of intensity during the worst moments.

I am often reminded of the child who studied with several teachers at the Harbor Conservatory, including myself. None of us seemed able to teach her. Although she was ten years old, she paid very little attention to what was being taught, reverting to such infantile behavior as baby talk and childish motions with her body and hands. She was apparently learning absolutely nothing. After experimenting with many approaches without success we came to the conclusion that she was either emotionally disturbed or had some minimal brain dysfunction or both. However, the mother refused to discuss this aspect. Since at previous lessons the child had asked to change to drum lessons, this was recommended to her mother. The wise mother rather angrily refused and requested a change in piano teachers. Quite reluctantly we decided to humor her and assigned an imaginative sensitive teacher who enjoyed working with "problem" children. Much to our astonishment the new teacher gained an immediate strong rapport with the child. She apparently sensed accurately what the child needed in the way of teacher relationship, and within a short time the child progressed very well indeed.

It is quite obvious that we other teachers had failed to give sufficient thought to establishing a relationship with this child. It did not occur to us that she was sabotaging her lessons because she did not trust us. As for myself, I had handled the problem purely from the clinical aspects, which certainly was constructive in itself since the child did prove to have perceptual difficulties. However, I had apparently overlooked such aspects as her fears, her anxieties or her distrust. On the other hand her new teacher had divined what the child needed in the way of a relationship. She had convinced the child that she cared about her and understood and sympathized with her problems. In short, the teacher placed herself completely on the child's side. By this means she won the child's trust, drew her out and inspired her to do her best.

After the bond of trust is established, the essential keyword is "respect". As long as the student feels he is respected by the teacher, he will be likely to build his musical foundation on healthy psychological grounds. His feelings and point of view should be an important part of any decision. He should be allowed to state his mind, speak freely, state his case, even if it includes criticism of the teacher, without fear of reprimand or reprisal.

For example, nine year old Edward came back for his lesson with his assignment well prepared, except for one thing. He had forgotten to look at the key signature! "I love the way you play it, Edward. It is exciting, but it sounds strange, something is different about it". Edward looked closely at the music, then noticed the two sharps in the key signature, and realized he had left them out throughout the piece. He became flustered, embarrassed and tears came to his eyes. "It was your fault, Mr. Lawrence, you didn't remind me!" "I didn't? How stupid of me, Edward. I'm so sorry. You see, even teachers are forgetful. Let's take care of that right now." Edward's tears turned to a smile and we reviewed key signatures. The omission failed to become a threat mainly because the teacher had respected Edward's little moment of anger, and had not permitted it to become an issue. Later on in the lesson, Edward said, out of a blue sky: "I shouldn't need to be reminded about key signatures, should I, Mr. Lawrence." "That day will come eventually, Edward". Thus the teacher's example of accepting responsibility for a "goof" had rubbed off on his student. The display of respect for Edward's feelings and in not holding him to account for his "signature" oversight in turn strengthened his respect for himself. As a result he was now able to accept responsibility for his own "goof".

Another keyword in the teacher-student relationship is "flexibility". This means doing away with rigid instructions and assignments. We help the child grow naturally if we encourage him to participate in planning and in making decisions. We help him even more when there are moments of conflict or anxiety, if we allow him the opportunity to face his problems and the room to overcome them; if we give him the flexibility to work problems through himself and *in his own time.*

Eleven year old Nina came to her lesson with her new assignment unprepared. "I don't like this piece, Mr. Lawrence, it's yukky so I didn't practice it." We both knew that she said this because she felt the piece was too difficult for her even though we had spent considerable preparation time on it at the previous lesson. Many times in the past she had found it difficult to take the first plunge since the piece always looked too hard. Once she was in the water, so to speak, it was easy sailing. However, she usually resisted even the slightest bit of pressure to make the initial effort.

"Too bad, it happens to be one of my favorites, but there is no reason why you have to like it. There are many pieces I don't like, either. Let's pick another one." Several compositions were examined and she chose one, and we worked on preparing it for the week's practicing.

The following week Nina came back with the *first* composition well prepared. "I decided I liked this one after all!" "What a delightful surprise!

You are sure it's not because I said I liked it?"
"Absolutely not. I just tried it again and could
hear that it was pretty, so I learned it." Of course,
the actual reason that Nina had decided on piece
number one was that it was more advanced than
piece number two. Left to her own devices, she
accepted the implied challenge I had presented
to her: you may, if you like, work on the easier
composition. The important point was that Nina
faced her difficulty in her own way and in her
own time. She had made the decision, not the
teacher, and in doing so she was better equipped
to handle "plunging" into the more difficult composition. By giving her flexibility to maneuver and
room to face her own indecision and evasion we
served two important purposes. She was assured
the teacher would care about and respect her regardless of which piece she played. Her self-esteem
had been strengthened by her own decision and
success in implementing it.

Beyond all of this the teacher will find himself
cast in many roles. He will be Friend, Confessor,
Advisor, Recipient of a child's "crush", Big Brother or Sister, Rescuer in troublesome times, etc.
Nevertheless, whatever the role, he makes one fact
unmistakably clear. He is always, first of all, the
Piano Teacher. On the other hand, when he finds
it necessary to be firm, stern, persistent, or even
angry with the student, the teacher must make it
clear, at the same time, that he loves, trusts, and
above all *respects* the child. Many teachers are
profoundly moved by the realization that the lesson
time may be the only time where the child has
the complete and total attention of an adult.

During the lesson, the adult is never called away or diverted from the child by other duties or interests. The involved teacher can only respect the overall effect this is bound to have on any child's life.

Paul Sheftel, in Clavier magazine, points out that though the piano teacher is not a therapist and does not have the same objectives as a therapist, there is, in one respect, a striking similarity between the professions—"In both settings the *relationship* is of paramount importance."[1] (Author's italics).

---

[1] Paul Sheftel, "The Piano Teacher as Psychotherapist." Clavier, Ap. 1977.

18
Suggestions for Innovations

IT IS HOPED THAT OUR OVERVIEW has indicated to the piano teacher the way the average piano student reacts and learns. It is hoped, further, that the teacher will find useful and effective the guidelines included in this book. However, even though the results show a considerable rise in student longevity and carryover, our experience at the Harbor Conservatory makes clear that much more can and must be done to raise the longevity and carryover percentages to still higher levels.

There are two areas outside of piano teaching per se, related to general policy, which we have followed with much success over the years. Teachers are urged to give them serious consideration for their own practice.

The first has to do with encouraging the student to study a second instrument in addition to the piano. The piano, rewarding instrument which it is, is primarily an instrument for *self-expression,* it is usually played alone, or for the pleasure of others (a very small percentage of amateurs use it for ensemble playing). However, a second instrument such as the violin, clarinet, or trumpet, is almost always played together with other instrumentalists. It is a sharing instrument. The student participates in an orchestra, band or small ensemble wherein he makes music together with several individuals and thereby becomes a member of the team making the total sound. Thus it is rewarding in another way, different from the piano. Add the two together and the student is enriched in music and music-making. There could be dramatic benefits from this. I base that conclusion on a very interesting statistic revealed in the CARRYOVER SURVEY. Seventy-three percent of students who played the piano *plus a second instrument* achieved carryover. Comparing this with the meager thirty-five percent carryover of students who played only the piano, we must seriously consider the possibility that the higher carryover percentages came as a *result* of the broader musical expression and wider variety in musical experience.

For these reasons, the piano teacher should recommend to the student, by the time he is nine or ten, that he choose a second instrument. Most public schools not only offer group instrumental music where the student may receive instruction without charge, but orchestral and band playing as well, where he may experience music-sharing. Of course, he may always elect to take individual lessons with a private teacher, if his parents can afford the added costs and he wishes to make faster, more detailed progress.

The second area of general policy has to do with the specific circumstances when a recommendation to *change* instruments would serve the student well. This is another option which we urge the teacher to consider.

Though it is our basic aim to teach the student so that he achieves sufficient music-making mastery for carryover into adulthood, it does not necessarily follow that the piano is the only means to that end. While it is true that the great majority of people prefer the piano to other instruments, there are those whose chances for carryover would be better via another instrument. For example, there is the student who is having too much difficulty learning to read two clefs simultaneously as required by piano. He might be far happier with an instrument like the flute, trumpet or clarinet, etc., which requires reading of a single clef. Then there is the student who has a "burning" desire to play a particular instrument, because for some reason it has a special appeal for him. He should be encouraged to study it. Finally, of course, there is the adolescent who may elect to drop the piano in favor of the guitar, as described in Chapter 10. The point is that when, in such instances, the teacher recommends a change of instrument, he contributes to the student's development and there will be a better chance for him to continue his music training and retain his momentum toward carryover.

*   *   *

Doubtless, the teacher could develop or create many other ideas which would affect carryover in a positive way. As examples, I offer two teaching plans for the reader's consideration. These are the Tandem Teaching Plan and the Re-enforcing Lesson Plan. So far as we know the first has never been tried among private teachers, though we use it exclusively at the Harbor Conservatory, and we have only recently begun to experiment with the second. We believe the innovative and daring teacher will find them of special interest and perhaps will even experiment with their implementation.

The Tandem Teaching Plan calls for five or more private teachers to band together as a team. Each teacher continues to operate in his own studio or in the student's home, as he has done in the past. Each teacher limits his teaching to a specific area of music training. This could be an area for which he is best trained, or at which he particularly enjoys working. The important thing is that each teacher coordinates his "specialty" with those of the other teachers of the team, for the benefit of the student. The program works like this: Mrs. A. favors beginning students. Mrs. B. loves to teach basic technique, sightreading and other skills, Mr. C. excels in teaching pop music, jazz and improvisation. Mr. D. is quite successful with helping problem children. And Mrs. E. does extremely well with more advanced, serious students. In Tandem Teaching the five or more teachers make a pact to revolve all students who apply to them according to the student's musical needs. For example, all beginning students are referred to Miss A. Of course, if it turns out to be a very busy group, there will be several teachers in Mrs. A.'s category, so the new student will be sure of a place with a beginning specialist. At the end of a pre-planned period, i.e., a year or two, the student will be promoted to Mrs. B. for sightreading and technical work. When Mrs. B. determines the time is ripe she will in turn promote the student to either the jazz teacher, the "problem" specialist, or the serious teacher, whichever will serve the student's needs best at that time.

From the student's point of view, the advantages of the Tandem Teaching Plan should immediately be obvious. When he reaches a certain point in his development he will be placed by his present teacher into the hands of a specialist who is geared to *advance his musical growth from the point just completed,* and to fulfill his particular musical needs of the moment. Compare this plan with the all too common example of the parent or student who decides to change teachers, only to find the new teacher does not "approve" of the child's past musical training and insists they start "from the beginning" again according to the new teacher's "special" methods. We have met children who have had as many as five teachers, and had started "from the beginning again" five different times! How discouraging this can be to the child!

In Tandem Teaching this waste is eliminated. The teachers, by virtue of being a team, know one another's methods and teaching patterns, and through consultations between them are prepared to move right on in the necessary educational direction. Furthermore, the child is bound to learn more from the teacher who is specialized in a specific area. In Tandem Teaching, the student has the advantage of several specialists, each devoted to contributing his share to the whole of the child's music training. In addition, the student has, for the first time, the opportunity of working with the "right" teacher at each critical stage of his development, and the prospects for longevity and carryover are thereby increased.

The advantages to the teacher are that his public image as an educator devoted to the student's musical welfare is enhanced, and he has the greater pleasure in his work because he spends more time on his chosen specialty.

We have followed the Tandem Teaching Plan at the Neighborhood Music School and The Harbor Conservatory for many years with much success. Admittedly, it is a relatively simple matter for a school to operate such a plan. The faculty of specialists is under one roof, and there is a Director to administer the flow of students moving from one teacher to another. The private teacher does not have these advantages. Yet I am convinced such a program could work very well in the private sector. It should serve both students and teachers well.

The second Plan has been tentatively designated the Re-enforcement Lesson Plan. At this writing we have experimented with a limited number of students for almost a year with a follow-up lesson the day after the regular lesson took place. The same lesson is repeated in the nature of a practice session. Although it has all of the characteristics of the original lesson, there are interesting aspects added. Apparently, a large portion of the instruction at the initial lesson does not penetrate completely, even when the teacher is under the impression that it does. Often children leave a lesson thinking they understand when in fact they don't. The Re-enforcement Lesson reveals these lapses and of course offers the opportunity to clarify them. The Re-enforcement Lesson also solidifies that which *did* penetrate well and the student grasps the newly learned concepts more firmly. We find that the student knows *how* to practice much more effectively than he did prior to the extra sessions. We also find that he has greater motivation and he seems to develop inner discipline with less effort.

However, we realize that this plan is quite difficult to implement since the logistics of teaching time do not lend themselves to such a program. We, of course, are going to continue to experiment with the concept, and hopefully, so will some of my readers.

These are but a few examples of how the teacher could seek and explore facets outside of music teaching itself which might help achieve longevity and carryover for the piano student.

19
Conclusion

THUS WE HAVE COME TO THE END of our profile of the piano student. Longevity in music-making can better be accomplished by understanding the child in his year by year growth and development in piano training, and accepting as a reality of life that fluctuations in achievement and behavioral attitudes are normal; by having an awareness of sibling rivalries; recognition of the tendency to favor one learning sense over the others; and, finally, insight into the student's personal problems. Factors also involved are parental re-education and teacher-student relationship. In addition, recommendations for the student to play a second instrument can add further strength to the longevity aspect of music training.

This overview of the piano student is only one point of view. It was formulated after much investigation and selection of applicable concepts from the various schools of thought in psychology and music education. To me it appears that the insights and approaches of Gesel, Piaget, Adler,

Thorndyke, Woodward and Curwin offer the soundest basis for our studies. We feel that this point of view has worked very well for us at the Neighborhood Music School and The Harbor Conservatory For Musical Growth. We trust it will do so for the reader.

However, the author is convinced that much more investigation, research and experimentation is required in order to understand better the developing child in relationship to music training, and so to improve our teaching. The study-results, observations and conclusions documented in these pages should be considered only a beginning. There is so much we do not yet know about learning processes in the child. We cannot even be sure that we are not hindering his music learning rather than furthering it. We must suspect that some of our answers are wrong when, as indicated in the CARRYOVER REPORT, we learn that *every self-taught person achieved carryover* (see APPENDIX). Every person who discontinued lessons after a short period and then proceeded to *teach himself*, plays currently! Of course, we may rationalize that he is more gifted, or more highly motivated. However, we cannot rule out the possibility that his success by implication is an indictment of music teaching. And we may well ask, did they, the self-taught, see or feel something about music teaching which we have missed? We refer the reader to the quote by Arthur Humphreys which appears at the end of the CARRYOVER REPORT in the APPENDIX.

Fortunately, the conscientious private piano teacher is one of the most searching of all professionals. He is rarely satisfied with the state of music teaching as it is. Seeking to learn more and to improve his teaching skills is a way of life with him. During the summer, throughout the country, we note the large enrollment of piano teachers at Piano Workshop Clinics, which emphasize new approaches and methods. The piano teacher apparently agrees with the comment made by Ekstein and Motto in their book, FROM LEARNING FOR LOVE TO LOVE OF LEARNING (Brunner/Hazel, N.Y. 1969) that "educators need . . . . a kind of creative industry matched by a constant sense of still not knowing enough, a kind of professional inferiority in the service of professional maturation."

The author believes that self-questioning of this type is healthy and indeed necessary if we are to improve our teaching. Thus our constant vigilant practice must be the continual investigation into our insights in children and how they learn, the persistent re-evaluation of our methods, of our teaching per se, as well as our goals. This book has been intended as an exercise in that practice.

Appendix

(The Carryover Report)[1]

Sidney J. Lawrence
Nadia Dachinger

Factors Relating to Carryover of Music Training into Adult Life

AccORDING TO the results of a recent study, the acquisition of skills—such as sightreading, improvising, and playing by ear—is an important factor necessary to the carryover of music training into adult life. The study demonstrated that at least 63 percent of the music students of the 1920's, 30's and 40's have not continued to play their instruments as adults. Self-taught musicians comprise the highest percentage of those who play today. The second highest percentage represents pianists who play other instruments as well, and the third highest is for string players. Pianists do not fare well, and neither do woodwind or brass players.

The authors conducted a survey during the spring of 1965 to investigate the long-range results of music instruction and factors controlling or affecting those results. Studies on carryover made during the past twenty years have concentrated solely on orchestral instrument training in the public schools.[1] In this study, the authors felt there was much to be gained by encompassing students of all instruments—including piano and guitar—whether they had been taught in public schools, music schools, or by private music teachers.

In conducting the survey, the authors sought to answer the following nine questions:

1. What have been the far-reaching effects of instrumental instruction?
2. How does the training in various instruments compare in the long range results?
3. Seen from an adult's viewpoint, in what specific ways has instrumental instruction been successful?
4. Which skills does the adult find most useful?

---

[1] "Bibliography of Research Studies in Music Education, 1949-1956," *Journal of Research in Music Education*, V, No. 2 (Summer 1957); and "Bibliography of Research Studies in Music Education, 1932-1948," *Music Education Research Council*, 1949.

[1] *Journal of Research In Music Education* XV, No.1 (1967) 23-31, Reprinted by permission of the *Journal of Research In Music Education*.

5. For how many adults has there been no carryover?

6. What factors contribute to or control musical carryover or the lack of it?

7. What relationship do factors like willingness to practice, consistency of practice, where music was studied, have to either success or failure of carryover?

8. Of what value were music lessons to those adults who studied music in their youth, but who do not play today?

9. Why do the respondents give their children music lessons?

RESEARCH PROCEDURE

To conduct the survey, the authors prepared a questionnaire covering general and specific questions relating to past instrumental training and present music-making activity of the subjects. Four nonprofit institutions in New York cooperated to make the subject sampling as broad economically and socially as possible. The participating schools were: a music school in the Bronx (estimated income of community residents, $4,000-$10,000); a music school in Croton-On-The Hudson (estimated community resident income, $10,000-$20,000); a community music and art center in Roslyn, Long Island (estimated community resident income, $15,000-$50,000); and the Harbor Conservatory for Musical Growth in Hewlett, the headquarters of the survey (high resident community income). The questionnaire was sent to the parents of the children enrolled in these institutions on the assumption that such parents were typical of those more likely to have received instrumental training in their youth, as compared with parents who were not paying for their children's music lessons. The questionnaire was mailed to 1,600 adults. Only those who had had musical training were asked to answer. Professionals who had any connection with performing, teaching, or composing music were excluded. Over 300 answers, 20.5 percent, of the original mailing were received. From those the authors tabulated the results listed in this report.

RESULTS

Through the survey, the following criteria were assessed: number of adults still playing their musical instruments; affect of parental attitudes and teaching emphasis on carryover; affect on carryover of place of study, regularity of lessons, willingness to practice and consistency of practice; how adults use their music-making; skill rated most important and self-appraisal of skills mastered; affect on carryover of stopping age, number of years of study, and sightreading ability; why subjects do not play their instruments today; reasons for giving their own children music lessons. Subjects were divided into two groups for the survey: those who play their instruments often or sometimes, the "P's," and those who play their instruments rarely or never, the "N's." For the most part, results

TABLE 1
ADULTS STILL PLAYING MUSICAL INSTRUMENTS

Instrument	P*	Percent	N*	Percent	Total
Piano	78	35	145	65	223
Piano plus other instrument	35	73	13	27	48
Strings**	20	61	13	39	33
Woodwinds	2	20	7	70	9
Brass			11	100	11
Percussion	1				1
Accordion	2		1		3
Total	138	37	190	73	328

*P = subject plays often or sometimes as an adult; N = subject plays rarely or never as an adult.

** Strings consisted of: violin, 18; cello, 4; guitar, 12; ukulele, 1; mandolin, 2; some subjects played more than one stringed instrument.

are tabulated separately for the P's and N's. A breakdown of the results of the survey follows.

In attempting to assess how many adults in the survey still play their musical instruments, 37 percent of the respondents proved to be P's, and 63 percent were N's (Table 1). Seventy percent of all who answered were female. Of these, more than 80 percent had studied piano or piano plus another instrument. Of the males, more than 40 percent had studied instruments other than the piano.

Twenty-five of the subjects were completely or partially self-taught. All play today. Eight piano, ten piano plus, and two string players were partially self-taught. Two piano, two string players, and one accordionist were completely self-taught.

Table 2 shows that the results of this questionnaire are reflections of the teaching emphasis and parental attitudes of the twenties and thirties

TABLE 2
STARTING DATE OF MUSIC LESSONS

Date	Piano		Piano Plus Other Instrument		Strings, Brass, Woodwinds		Total Answered
	P%	N%*	P%	N%	P%	N%	
Before 1920							7
1920's	39	61	70	10	60	30	72
1930's	41	59	60	40	20	70	125
1940's	38	62	62	38	20	60	46
1950's							3

*P = subject plays often or sometimes as an adult; N = subject plays rarely or never as an adult.

and, to a lesser degree, of the forties. The twenties was a prosperous period, the thirties a depression period, and the forties a war period; yet, it is significant that with the wide difference in economic eras, there is little difference in the carryover ratio.

Factors Affecting Carryover

Table 3 examines the various places of study. In this sampling, in general, there proves to be little relationship to the long range results. It should be noted that many individuals had more than one teacher and had studied at both a music school and with private teachers, and at home as well as at a teacher's studio. About 10 percent seemed to have received instruction at public schools, and about 18 percent had some private music school experience.

Since irregularity in music lessons could be a cause for discouragement and consequent dropout, the affect of regularity of lessons on carryover was evaluated. Results showed that a small percentage of students were involved with irregular lessons, and they seemed more inclined to use their music as adults rather than those who had had regular instruction.

Willingness to practice showed no apparent relationship to carryover. Of the former piano students, 43 percent of the P's practiced willingly, 44 percent were constantly reminded to practice, and 13 percent were forced to practice. On the other hand, 40 percent of the N's practiced willingly, 46 percent were constantly reminded, and 14 percent were forced to practice. Comparison of these results with other instrumental categories finds similar parallels.

Consistency in practice did not prove to be a factor which influenced carryover. In piano, for example, 60 percent of those who play today practiced regularly, while 68 percent of those who do not play today also practiced regularly. On the other hand, 37 percent of those who play today practiced irregularly, while 30 percent of those who do

TABLE 3
RELATIONSHIP OF PLACE OF STUDY TO CARRYOVER

Studied at	Piano		Piano plus Other		Strings		Woodwinds		Brass		Miscel- laneous	
	P	N*	P	N	P	N	P	N	P	N	P	N
Public School	1	1	8	3	3	1	1	4	0	8	0	0
Private Music School	9	13	15	4	0	6	0	0	0	2	0	0
Private Teacher	73	134	32	12	10	12	1	2	0	3	2	1
At Home	34	52	21	11	8	8	2	1	0	2	1	1
At Studio	57	112	20	6	5	9	1	1	0	1	2	0

*P = subject plays often or sometimes as an adult; N = subject plays rarely or never as an adult.

TABLE 4

SELF APPRAISAL OF SKILLS ATTAINED

Skills		Piano		Piano Plus Other		Strings		Woodwinds		Brass	
		P%	N%	P%	N%	P%	N%	P%	N%	P%	N%
Sightreading	G*	20	3	32	9	54		20			9
	F	61	23	44	40	23	27	20			9
	U	19	75	25	52	23	73	60			32
Improvisation	G	4	5	16	8			15			9
	F	16	4	33		50	25				
	U	80	92	47	92	50	75	85			91
Accompanying	G	10		25		28		20			
	F	35	11	38	17	57	33				18
	U	55	89	38	83	12	67	80			82
Interpretation	G	20	15	38	17	36		17			9
	F	36	24	25	22	45	33	33			9
	U	45	75	38	60	19	66	50			82
Memory	G	19	14	25	0	9		16			
	F	21	22	49	40	55	14	16			27
	U	60	64	33	62	36	86	67			67
Ensemble	G	5		28	9	28		20			
	F	9	1	24	17	55	22	20			27
	U	85	99	48	94	18	88	60			73

High	Sight. 81%	Mem. 36%	Sight. 76%	Sight. 48%	Sight. 77%	Acc. 33%	Inter. 50%	Mem. 27%

*Key: G = Good; F = Fair; U = Unsatisfactory

not play today practiced irregularly. Similar results occurred for the P's and N's in other categories. It appears, from this sampling, that consistency in practicing is no guarantee for carryover.

Skills Related to Long Range Playing

The P's were asked to indicate in which of the following ways they used their music training today: playing in ensemble; playing in "pop" ensemble; sightreading; improvising; playing by ear; accompanying; playing by memory. Results showed that, with the exception of string players who play more in ensembles, sightreading is the most important skill. However, most of these P's used music in more than one way.

When the respondents were asked which skill they rated as most important, the majority selected sightreading first and improvisation second, thus verifying previous findings.[2] Significantly N's also rated sightreading as most important.

In Table 4 the P's report a high percentage of "good" and "fair" self rating in sightreading. The N's on the other hand report a strikingly

² Kuersteiner, "Aims and Objectives of Piano Study," *MTNA Convention Report*, 1944; and Lawrence, *A Guide To Remedial Sightreading For the Piano Student* (Hewlett, New York: Workshop Music Publications, 1964), pp. 70-73.

low level of self appraisal for the same item. They stressed other skills to the neglect of sightreading: the pianists concentrated on memory, string players on accompaniment and interpretation. Apparently the mastery of sightreading is an important factor which affects the student's chances of playing in adulthood.

Additional Factors Affecting Carryover

Music teachers often claim that the majority of students drop music lessons between the ages of twelve and fourteen. Did subjects in this survey who stopped lessons at or before age fourteen return to music playing later? For the most part they did not. However, the drop-out age level is apparently of some significance. Fifty-four percent of the P's played beyond the age of fifteen, while 46 percent dropped out at age fourteen or before. If we compare this with the N's, the ratio is 20:80, a considerable difference. In each of the remaining instrumental categories this ratio checked out. Fourteen seems to be the age beyond which the student must pass if he is to have a better chance to play in adulthood.

TABLE 5
RELATIONSHIP OF YEARS OF MUSIC STUDY TO CARRYOVER

Number of years studied	Piano		Piano plus other		Strings, woodwind, brass combined	
Group I	P	N	P	N	P	N
1	3	8	1		2	6
2	8	46	3	2	1	4
3	9	35	4	2	1	9
Total	20	89	8	4	4	19
Percent of both groups	36	67	22	30	18	68
Group II	P	N	P	N	P	N
4	16	23	4	4	6	4
5	9	17	5		2	7
6	8	4	3	1	3	1
7	4	2	3	1	2	
8	7	10	2	1	2	
9 plus	12	1	12	2	3	1
Total	56	57	29	9	18	13
Percent of both groups	64	33	78	70	82	32
Mean	5.3	3.8	5.3	5	5.2	3.2

Table 5 indicates that there is a direct significance between the number of years of study and carryover. In order to examine the number of years of training involved as related to carryover, the respondents were divided into two groups. Students who had a maximum of three years of study were compared with those who had a minimum of four, and in turn both categories were related to long range playing. In the

152

case of piano and combined instruments, the P's who had studied four years or more scored higher than the N's who had studied for the same length of time. Only in the "piano plus other instruments" was the ratio different in the N's.

However, the following question then arises: what about the P's who had played three years and less? There were 36 percent in piano, 22 percent in piano plus, and 18 percent in the combined other instruments. There must be some other factor involved which kept them playing their musical instruments through adulthood. Achievement of skills was supected.

Results showed that a student whose training is limited to two or three years has a chance for carryover only if he has learned to sightread, improvise, or play by ear in that period. Re-examination of self appraisal of sightreading in those who had studied three years or less brought these results: in piano fourteen P's sightread at least fairly well as against six who read poorly. The latter six either improvise or play by ear On the other hand, only nine N's sightread at least fairly well as against eighty who could neither sightread, improvise, nor play by ear. The remaining ratios were similar (although the numbers were smaller).

The N's were asked why they do not play and to select the reasons from those listed in Table 6. As can be seen from this table, the greatest common reason for not playing as adults is the lack of sufficient skill.

TABLE 6
REASONS WHY ADULTS STOPPED PLAYING INSTRUMENTS

Reason for not playing	Piano	Piano plus Other	Strings	Woodwinds	Brass
Lack of time	6%	18%	8%		
Lack of interest	9		15	43%	26%
Aversion to playing	3			14	
Has forgotten how	17	18	23		
Never achieved sufficient skill	65	37	54	43	74
Lack of instrument		7			

When the N's were asked what value music instruction had for them, 58 percent felt they had received some value from their training even though they do not play as adults. Forty-two percent felt it was a waste. Almost half of these subjects, in other words, found absolutely no value in their music training.

Reasons for Giving Children Music Lessons

More than two-thirds of the subjects give their children music lessons now because they feel it is a necessary part of their educational development. Less than one-third give them to the children because the children request them. The reasoning of the first group appears to be that children need guidance and that such important decisions cannot be left to them. The second group seems to feel that music playing is not necessarily for everyone and it is up to the child to want lessons. In a breakdown of the P's and N's, twenty-nine of the P's give their children music lessons because they are requested while eighty-one P's make this decision themselves. Thirty-eight N's give their children lessons upon request while sixty-seven N's make such decisions themselves.

Of the entire group giving their children lessons now, 69 percent of parents from both the highest and lowest economic levels feel they should make and carry out the decisions to provide the lessons. In each economic group, 31 percent have given the lessons at the request of the children. Percentages in all instances are identical. Apparently the rationale behind parental decisions is not affected by economic and sociological differences.

CONCLUSIONS

In considering reasons for the large percentage of those who fail to achieve carryover in music-making, there are several factors which cannot be measured or sampled in a survey such as this. Without question, psychological factors influenced some students and there must have been some whose lack of carryover was also affected by the problems in learning development. However, this survey does point to some general areas which could affect long-range playing.

The evidence that childhood willingness to practice, consistency in practicing, and the like has little relationship to carryover in adulthood may come as a surprise to many teachers and educators. Probably, each student's reaction to music study and practicing is a variable which moves from high enthusiasm to boredom, indifference or outright hostility, and depends upon the age, social and psychological factors in the student's life, and his musical needs at any given period. Although willingness and consistency in practice may have little bearing on carryover, experimentation in guiding students during "low" periods could prove of value in diminishing the "quitting" tendency. This in turn would raise the carryover percentage.

Particularly interesting is the fact that every person who was self-taught plays currently. Has the partially self-taught person achieved carryover because he is more gifted than others? Or is this success, by implication, an indictment of music teaching? Arthur F. Humphreys of State University College, Crane Department of Music, Potsdam, New York, asks, "Inadvertent though it may be, is it possible that the music learning opportunities of children are hampered and sometimes even ruined by the music specialist himself? . . . could it be that the music specialist sometimes actually prevents music learning in children?"[3] Further exploration of why the self-taught person leaves formal training and how he teaches himself may be of great benefit to the teaching profession.

[3] Arthur F. Humphreys, "The Music Educator: A Part of the Answer or a Part of the Problem," *Music Educators Journal*, 51 (January 1965), 72.

Another significant factor arising from this study is the need to have students study the piano *plus* another instrument. The indication is that there is a far greater chance for carryover in this instance. One must ask, however: does the student who learns to play the piano plus another instrument do so because he has stronger musical urges, motivation, and/or talent? Or, will a well-planned program stressing "piano plus" bring about a higher percentage of carryover? The authors are convinced that while the former is probably a contributing factor, the latter course offers possibility and promise. Investigation, research, and experimentation along these lines are indicated.

Viewing the lack of carryover in woodwinds and brass players, it can readily be seen that proportionately only a small group is represented here. Certain factors cannot be measured or sampled, such as the question of keeping the "lip" in playable condition and also the problem of where to play and with whom (problems which are not so acute with the pianist, violinist, or guitarist). However, there is cause for concern if the present rate of carryover among woodwind and brass players continues.

Today the number of woodwind and brass students has multiplied greatly, primarily because more public schools throughout the country make the study of orchestral instruments an important part of their educational program. In addition, teaching techniques, approaches, and know-how have improved greatly. These factors should contribute to improved carryover for the future, although it appears that more investigation is called for in this area of instrumental training.

The basic weakness in piano training of the 1920-1950 period as related to carryover appears to have been the lack of emphasis on sightreading skills. This factor was insufficiently stressed. In addition, both teachers and parents were unaware that it was important to keep the student at the piano until he has mastered sightreading and other neglected skills, such as improvising, at least to a workable degree.

This survey mirrors the level of carryover which resulted from teaching emphasis and parental attitudes of the twenties, thirties, and forties. The challenge before us now is: will our present teaching goals and areas of emphasis raise this level of carryover?

Harbor Conservatory for Musical Growth
Massapequa Public Schools, New York

155

Recommended
Bibliography

ADLER, Alfred—UNDERSTANDING HUMAN NATURE, 1927, Greenberg, N.Y.

ADLER, Alfed—PATTERNS OF LIFE, 1930, Cosmopolitan Book Co., N.Y.

ADLER, Alfred—SCIENCE OF LIVING, 1928, Garden City Pub. Co., Garden City, N.Y.

ALMY, Millie, et al—YOUNG CHILDREN'S THINKING, 1967, Teachers College Press, N.Y.

ANASTASI, A.—PSYCHOLOGICAL TESTING, 1961, Macmillan Co., N.Y.

BALDWIN, Alfred—THEORIES OF CHILD DEVELOPMENT, 1968, John Wiley & Son, N.Y.

BETTELHEIM, Bruno—CHILDREN OF THE DREAM, 1968, The Macmillan Co., London.

BRUNER, Jerome S.—TOWARD A THEORY OF INSTRUCTION, 1966, Oxford University Press, N.Y.

BRUNER, Jerome S.—BEYOND INFORMATION

GIVEN (Ed. Anglon), 1973, W.W. Norton & Co., N.Y.

CADY, Calvin Brainard—MUSIC-EDUCATION, 1902, Clayton F. Summy Co., Chicago, Il.

COLEMAN, Satis N.—YOUR CHILD'S MUSIC, 1939, John Day Co., N.Y.

CURWIN, Mrs. Spencer J.—PSYCHOLOGY APPLIED TO MUSIC TEACHING, 1900, J. Curwin & Sons, London, G. Schirmer, N.Y. distr.

DARAZ, A. & S. Jay—SIGHT AND SOUND (Kodaly-Teacher's Manuel), 1965, Boosey & Hawks, Oceanside, N.Y.

DINKMEYER, Don & Rudolf DRIEKRUS—ENCOURAGING CHILDREN TO LEARN, 1965, Prentice-Hall, Englewood Cliffs, N.J.

DRAKE, R. M.—MANUAL FOR THE DRAKE MUSICAL APTITUDE TESTS (rev. ed), 1957, Science Research Assn., Chicago.

EKSTEIN, Rudolf and Rocco L. MOTTO—FROM LEARNING FOR LOVE TO LOVE OF LEARNING, 1969 Brunner/Mazel, N.Y.

ELKIND, David and John H. FLAVELL—STUDIES IN COGNITIVE DEVELOPMENT, 1969, Oxford University Press, N.Y.

ELLIOT, Grace Loucks—UNDERSTANDING THE ADOLESCENT GIRL, 1930, Henry Holt, N.Y.

FORER, Lucille, with Henry STILL—THE BIRTH ORDER FACTOR, 1976, David McKay Co., N.Y.

FURTH, Hans G.—PIAGET AND KNOWLEDGE, 1969, Prentice-Hall, Englewood Cliffs, N.J.

GARDNER, R. W. & A. MORIARTY—PERSONALITY DEVELOPMENT AT PRE-ADOLESCENCE, 1968, University of Washington, Seattle.

GESEL, Arnold & Francis L. ILG, et al—THE CHILD FROM FIVE TO TEN, 1946 Harper and Bros., N.Y.

HALL, D. & A. WALTER—ORFF-SCHULWERK —MUSIC FOR CHILDREN, Schott Music Co. Assn., Music Pub., N.Y.

KAUFMAN, Lloyd—SIGHT AND MIND, 1974, Oxford University Press, N.Y.

KREVIT, William—MUSIC FOR YOUR CHILD, 1946, Dodd, Mead & Co., N.Y.

KWALWASSER—KWALWASSER MUSIC TALENT TEST, 1953, Mills Music, N.Y.

LAWRENCE, Sidney J.—REMEDIAL SIGHT-READING FOR THE PIANO STUDENT, 1964, Workshop Music Teaching Pub., Hewlett, N.Y.

LAWRENCE, Sidney J.—CHALLENGES IN PIANO TEACHING, 1978, Workshop Music Teaching Pub., Hewlett, N.Y.

LAWRENCE, Sidney J.—THIS BUSINESS OF MUSIC PRACTICING, (Pamphlet), 1968, Workshop Music Teaching Pub., N.Y.

LAWRENCE, Sidney J.—EVERYONES MUSICAL, Psychologically Speaking, 1946, Clayton F. Summy, Chicago.

LEHMAN, Paul R—TESTS AND MEASUREMENTS IN MUSIC, 1968, Prentice-Hall, Englewood Cliffs, N. J.

LUNDEN, Robert W.—AN OBJECTIVE PSY-

CHOLOGY OF MUSIC, 1967, Ronald Press Co., N.Y.

MURRAY, M.–ORFF-SCHULWERK–MUSIC FOR CHILDREN, Schott Music Co. Assn. Music Pub., N.Y.

MURSEL, J.L.–THE PSYCHOLOGY OF MUSIC, 1937, W.W. Norton Co., N.Y.

PEARCE, Joseph Hilton–MAGICAL CHILD, 1977, E. P. Dutton, N.Y.

PIAGET, Jean–et al–PLAY AND DEVELOPMENT, 1972, W.W. Norton, N.Y.

PIAGET, Jean & Barbel INHELDER,–MEMORY AND INTELLIGENCE, 1973, Basic Bks, N.Y.

PIAGET, Jean–THE CHILD AND REALITY, 1973, Grossman, N.Y.

PIAGET, Jean–THE GRASP OF CONSCIOUSNESS, 1976, Harvard University Press, N.Y.

PIAGET, Jean–Ed. GRUBER & VONICHE–THE ESSENTIAL PIAGET, 1977, Basic Bks, N.Y.

PIAGET, Jean–Ed. FLAVEL–DEVELOPMENTAL PSYCHOLOGY OF JEAN PIAGET, 1963, D. Van Nostrand & Co., Princeton, N.J.

SCHOEN, M.–THE PSYCHOLOGY OF MUSIC, 1940, Ronald Press, N.Y.

SEASHORE, Carl E.–PSYCHOLOGY OF MUSICAL TALENT, 1919, Silver, Burdett & Co.

SILBERMAN, Charles E.–CRISES IN THE CLASSROOM, 1970, Random House, N.Y.

SPAETH, Sigmund–FIFTY YEARS OF MUSIC, 1959, Fleet Co., N.Y.

SPAETH, Sigmund—IMPORTANCE OF MUSIC, 1963, Fleet Co., N.Y.

SWISHER, Walter Samuel—PSYCHOLOGY FOR THE MUSIC TEACHER, 1927, Oliver Ditson Co., N.Y.

THORNDYKE, Edward L.—EDUCATIONAL PSYCHOLOGY, 1924, Teachers College, N.Y.

WOODWARD, Robert S.—PSYCHOLOGY, 1921, Henry Holt, N.Y.